YOUR
DO-ANYTHING
KITCHEN

FOOD52

YOUR DO-ANYTHING
KITCHEN

The trusty guide to a smarter,
tidier, happier space

Editors of Food52
Photographs by James Ransom
Illustrations by Nicole Belcher

TEN SPEED PRESS
California | New York

CONTENTS

Introduction

If you've ever cooked while camping—with nothing more than a heavy skillet over the campfire grates and a jug of water leaning against the nearest tree—you know that it's possible to make a homey, functional kitchen just about anywhere.

You can make a kitchen in a college dorm room, with a triple stack of storage bins for a pantry and some thrift-store mixing bowls and spoons. You can make one in a shoebox apartment with a single burner and mini fridge, in a big farmhouse with what feels like an acre of counter space, and anywhere in between. It doesn't need to be shaped a certain way or have a certain look; you don't have to install special cabinets or plot out renovations. With a hunger for good food, a roll-up-your-sleeves attitude, and a few key tools, a great kitchen emerges.

We're here to help you make your own great kitchen, plain and simple—whether you're starting from scratch or hoping to shake up your well-loved space. We want your kitchen to be somewhere you'll do a lot of cooking and just as much living. After all, isn't it the first place we hit in the morning, and the last place we turn out the lights before heading to bed? Not to mention all the time we spend there making toast and tea; putting the finishing touches on a birthday cake; or standing in front of the refrigerator, door open, looking for a late-night snack.

To guide you to that kitchen where you can do all that (and then some), we've created this mighty little handbook. It's packed with tips, tools, and strategies of all kinds, backed up by ten years of smarts from the Food52 test kitchen and our community of trusted home cooks. And since cooking is always more fun with friends, we've brought in some longtime favorite voices in food—cookbook authors, chefs, bakers, and more—who are, above all, devoted home cooks. We'll take a moment to peek into their kitchens, stand at their elbows, and learn just what makes their cheerful, delicious spaces their own.

This is a book for old hands and newbies alike, for the executive and sous chefs among us, for bakers and cooks, for big kitchens and little ones. We hope you'll turn to it when it's time to buy your first pan or upgrade your standby; when you're looking to stock your new home's kitchen or reignite your love for cooking. We hope this book sends you racing to fling open your cabinets with new determination. Most of all, we hope it helps make your kitchen feel like home.

—Amanda Hesser & Merrill Stubbs,
  cofounders of Food52

How to Use This Book

Think of this book as a letter of recommendation, a can-do manual, and a friendly voice to answer those tricky cooking questions that pop up every now and then. Chapter by chapter, you'll get rundowns on the tools you'll need to tackle any recipe, and the fridge and pantry goods to stock for a new world of on-a-whim meals (think bake-sale jam bars, olive oil-y focaccia, and pantry dinners galore). You'll learn our tricks for organizing everything and keeping it that way (yes, even your rambling spice collection); for finding both the adventure and the ease in cooking; and, finally, for cleaning it all up at the end—even the tricky baked-on stuff.

Within each chapter, we'll walk through all the main components of your kitchen: your workspace; your tools; and your pantry, fridge, and freezer. And at the end of the chapter, we'll give you a game plan to put the things you've learned into practice. We're talking shopping guides, checklists, and strategies of all sorts, to keep you on track when you get off and running.

You can turn to this book to:

- Outfit your drawers and cabinets like a test-kitchen cook (see page 14).

- Pare back your kitchen (see page 28) and donate what you no longer need (see page 87).

- Stock your kitchen tool kit with all the essentials for a couple hundred dollars or less (see page 30).

- Boost your everyday cooking with a stable of multipurpose ingredients (see page 47).

- Make soup from a stone—or just six really good meals, all from your pantry staples (see pages 44–46).

- Get your produce to last just a little bit longer (see page 54).

- Finally wrangle your food-storage containers in an order that makes sense (see page 75).

- Sort through your freezer (see page 82), really clean it (see page 125), and harness its power (see page 85).

- Learn the knife skills that'll take you from a mince to a mirepoix and everywhere in between (see pages 95–97).

- Become a kitchen-efficiency expert, like a seasoned restaurant chef (see page 107).

- Spruce up your whole kitchen from top to bottom, without using a single harsh chemical (see page 120).

- Break up the cleaning with a routine you can lean on (see page 143).

- Make the kitchen your very favorite place in the house (see page 26).

Our Kitchen & Home Wisdom

Whether we're whipping up waffles or washing dishes, setting the table or twirling spaghetti, we believe in eating thoughtfully and living joyfully. These ideas guide us in the kitchen and the rest of the home.

HOW YOU EAT IS HOW YOU LIVE.

We shop for, organize, and design our homes with the same care we put into cooking and eating—from taking the time to source ingredients we love to preparing and enjoying them.

SIMPLICITY IS THE NAME OF THE GAME.

What's beautiful (and delicious) should also be accessible, and some of our favorite ingredients and solutions are the simplest. All that matters is that *you* love it.

BUY FEWER, BETTER-QUALITY THINGS.

Whether food items or home goods, it's better to have a little of something you use often and will continue to cherish than a lot of something you don't love and won't use. Our wooden butcher block was a solid investment, but it's the only one we have—and it sees a *lot* of our daily dinner prep.

WASTE NOT.

Thoughtful consumption is the name of the game. We try to buy and cook only what we need, get creative with leftovers, and clean up with an eye toward eco-friendliness—meaning with as few chemicals and single-use anythings as possible.

SHOP SMALL.

We're talking buying from farmers, artisans, mom-and-pops, and food co-ops. When we have the option to support independent makers, we do.

COOK AT HOME AS MUCH AS YOU CAN.

Making a meal in the comfort of your own kitchen is one of life's greatest pleasures. Cooking is one of the most meaningful things anyone can do—for the environment, for your creativity, for bringing people together.

ANYBODY CAN COOK AND COOK WELL.

Even if you can't quite boil water or you always seem to burn your toast (hey—us, too), the tools and know-how in these chapters will inspire you to get cooking. To the kitchen!

CHAPTER 1

Setting Up

Let's say you want to go on a road trip—cross-country! You'll need a reliable car and a tank full of gas. You'll want a map you can trust, some time, patience, and a good playlist.

Now, let's say the road trip is actually a cooking journey. The car is your kitchen, and that tank of gas is your kitchen tool kit. And the trusty map? This chapter. Here, you'll find the crop of tools needed for nearly any recipe, plus the essentials for serving and enjoying what you cook (and saving it for later). As we get on our way, outfitting the kitchen little by little, we hope you'll add your own handy favorites and feel ready to take on the road.

Your Tools

When it comes to picking tools, we like to balance super-utilitarian with super-lovely. Tools that'll last forever, feel good in hand, and wink at us from the shelf or drawer? That's the stuff that has our name all over it. With kitchen tools, having fewer, higher-quality pieces is better than having too many unitaskers or special-occasion items that we don't reach for often. These go-tos will make cooking a heck of a lot easier—and more fun.

Tools fall into a few categories: for snipping, slicing, and mixing (knives, small appliances, handheld tools, and the like); for cooking, baking, and other kitchen wizardry (pots and pans and bakeware); and for serving, sharing, and nibbling (what the eating happens *on*). In each category, you'll find the **Must-Haves** that we couldn't cook without; you'll also find the **Nice-to-Haves** that broaden our kitchen's horizons (or simply speed up dinner). But it's not all work. We also call out the "tools" whose main job is to make you smile. That's a big part of being in the kitchen!

Knives: Making the Cut

A great knife can help you whip up just about anything—a shaved salad, a spatchcocked chicken, a hearty hash, and beyond. You'll use it more than any other tool. In general, we recommend knives with a solid, weighty stainless-steel or carbon-steel blade and a handle that feels nice in hand, whether plastic or wood. We're here to help you pick the right shapes and sizes for your cooking. (Psst: Check out Your Kitchen Cheat Sheet on page 148 for any measurement conversions you may need.)

Must-Haves

- **Chef's knife:** A true workhorse, this large knife has a broad, sharp blade for doing a whole mess of kitchen tasks. Choose between a Western-style chef's knife (with a slightly curved edge) and a Japanese-style santoku knife (a bit thinner, with a flat edge). We find 8- to 10-inch blades to be the most versatile.

- **Kitchen shears:** These can break down a raw chicken, snip fresh herbs, cut up a pizza, and lots more. Bonus points for blades that come apart for thorough cleaning.

- **Knife block, magnetic rack, or blade covers:** Instead of sticking knives straight into the drawer, where they'll quickly dull, consider using a countertop knife block or wall-mounted magnetic rack. If you do like your knives drawer-side (maybe you want them well out of the way of young kids or a rascally pet cat), try an in-drawer knife organizer or hardy blade covers. These helpers will protect your knives and you.

- **Paring knife:** Small, sharp, and light, this little one (3 to 5 inches!) is all about the details—hulling strawberries, scoring pie dough, deveining shrimp, and more.

- **Serrated knife:** This sturdy blade with small serrated grooves won't hesitate against a crisp crust, a tender tomato, or a delicate-crumbed cake. Go for one 10 inches long.

Nice-to-Haves

- **Cleaver:** A definite for at-home butchers. Look for one with a heavy handle and blade.

- **Honing steel and/or whetstone:** Sharp knives are safe knives, thanks to regular care. A honing steel realigns the "teeth" of the knife to help spruce up your blade in the short term, while a whetstone will give you a true sharpening. (If you don't have either of these, keep your friendly neighborhood knife sharpener—or hardware store—on speed dial.)

- **Mini serrated knife:** This 4½-incher is an ace for soft fruits, like peaches, stubborn-skinned citrus, or a log of frozen cookie dough.

WHERE IN THE WORLD IS MY KNIFE FROM?

Many countries are known for their knife craftsmanship, but the knives you'll see most often are German and Japanese. **German knives** are made of a thicker, softer steel than **Japanese knives**, which are made of a hard, thin, brittle steel that requires skilled sharpening. For an all-purpose or beginner's knife, go German. If you're an experienced cook with a trusted sharpener (or can sharpen yourself), go Japanese.

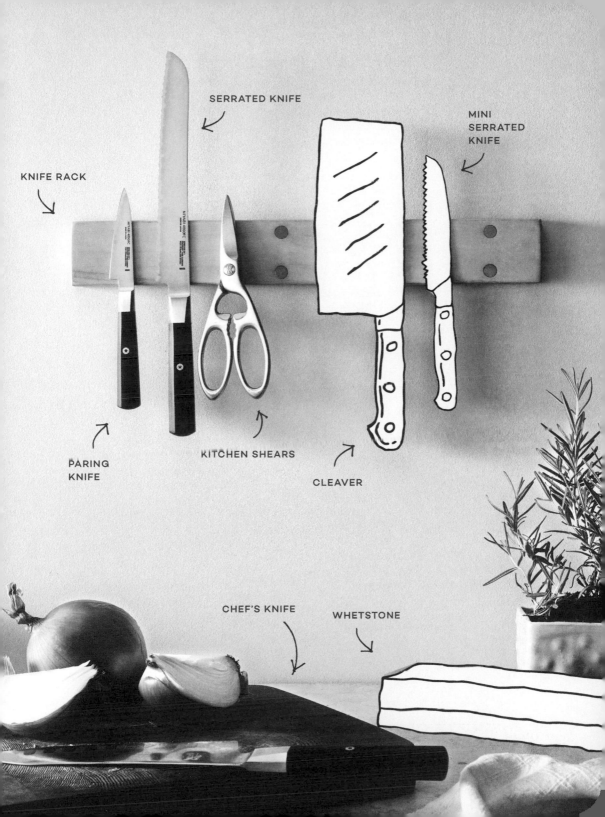

SERRATED KNIFE

MINI SERRATED KNIFE

KNIFE RACK

PARING KNIFE

KITCHEN SHEARS

CLEAVER

CHEF'S KNIFE

WHETSTONE

Cutting Boards: Join the Block Party

Almost all good cooking starts with honest chopping and slicing on a cutting board. We gravitate toward models without extra bells and whistles and keep a range of sizes: at least two large ones (12 by 18 inches, minimum) for most big jobs, and a little one (say, 6 by 8 inches) for cutting up a quick snack. (Psst: Check out Your Kitchen Cheat Sheet on page 148 for any measurement conversions you may need.)

Our Faves

- **Wooden or bamboo boards:** These go-tos are easy on knives and on the eyes, though they can be an investment and require some regular care. You can't go wrong with solid maple boards, but eco-friendly bamboo boards are a little friendlier on the wallet.

- **Plastic boards:** These are cheap, easy to clean, and kind to your knives; we always have a stack of them and love being able to throw 'em in the dishwasher after a particularly messy job. We prefer shock-absorbing solid plastic boards to flexible plastic sheets, which are less sturdy and more difficult to chop on comfortably.

- **Wooden butcher block:** If you have the space and budget, an extra-large (around 24 by 18 inches) and thick (1½ inches) chopping block is a handsome, near-indestructible statement piece. Whether a stand-alone block or part of your countertop, these get special designation. We love them for all the reasons we love wooden boards—looks, durability, and friendliness to knives. If you're able to budget a bit more for one of these beauts, you'll be amply rewarded.

No-Ways

- **Glass, slate, and marble boards:** They might look pretty, but cutting on them is like buying an express ticket to Dull Knife City. Save these for serving (hello, bountiful cheese plate!) instead.

WHAT IF I'M CUTTING MEAT?

Contrary to what you might have heard, plastic and wooden boards are equally good for meat. Wood is naturally antimicrobial (cool!) and, of course, is nice to look at—though plastic is easier to clean in the dishwasher. Regardless, if you cook meat often, keep one dedicated, durable board that you can consistently put through the cleaning wringer (see page 130 to learn how to remove any stains or smells that come your board's way).

The Cutting Board Our Community Helped Make

When we were designing our own dream cutting board for our Five Two line, we asked 10,000 home cooks about their essential features. Boy, did they have some great ideas.

They love a large, durable board with ample room for chopping . . .

. . . that's handsome enough to moonlight as a serving platter . . .

. . . with a deep juice-catching groove on one side (and a smooth reverse) . . .

. . . that's easy to lift (phew).

Small Appliances: The Magic Makers

These little machines are where so much of the transformation happens in the kitchen—but for most of your cooking, you'll just need a few things. Here are the zippers, zappers, and whirlers that earn their keep in our homes—and still leave our countertops uncluttered. (Psst: Check out Your Kitchen Cheat Sheet on page 148 for any measurement conversions you may need.)

Must-Haves

- **Stand or handheld electric mixer:** If you're a baker, your mixer is practically an extension of your body. Spring for a stand mixer (like the classic, near-synonymous KitchenAid) or go for the smaller, budget-friendlier hand mixer (which can't do quite everything a stand mixer can but makes light work of mixing and whipping all the same).

- **Food processor:** The giver of hummus, pesto, and quick-shredded cheese or vegetables— we love this machine and want to shout it from the rooftops! Pick one that has a capacity of at least 10 cups and comes with an all-purpose blade, a feeding tube, and a detachable shredding disc accessory that usually accompanies new models.

- **Caffeine machine (and accessories) of choice:** Teapot? French press? Auto-drip? Burr grinder? Buy whatever you need to get your fix.

Nice-to-Haves

- **Blender:** A food processor can do much of the work of a blender—but a blender really is king for liquids. Go for one with a capacity of at least 56 ounces; buy a high-powered version if you're a smoothie aficionado.

- **Immersion blender:** Great for lovers of creamy soups and homemade mayo.

- **Microwave, toaster, and/or toaster oven:** These are inessential tools to some, but couldn't-live-without-'ems to others. We'll let you be the judge on these shortcutters. Pick ones that are easy to clean, without too many extra parts.

- **Mini (3- to 5-cup) food processor:** This little one is great for smaller jobs that don't warrant the big processor, like chopping a handful of nuts or making a salsa verde.

- **Mortar and pestle:** Get a heavy marble or granite model with a large bowl that gives you room to work. (Alternatively, a small electric grinder is a good pick.)

- **Slow cooker, pressure cooker, or a combination multicooker:** The 6-quart size is a good all-purpose option. Use these for quicker-than-quick cooked beans and lentils; set-it-and-forget-it stews, chilis, and braises; and much more.

- **Stove-top or electric kettle:** Your pick for hot water, fast. A goosenecked model is great for extra-precise pour-over coffee.

Unnecessary-but-Lovable Unitaskers

- **Ice-cream maker:** For lovers of rocky road cones and slushy cocktails alike, we'd happily recommend either the frozen canister-style or a superluxe self-refrigerating model.

- **Juicer:** An easy-to-clean machine (read: dishwasher-safe parts) with an extra-large pulp bin will serve you well. If you're new to juicing, consider a more affordable centrifugal model, which uses heat to extract the juice; cold-press juicers are a bit pricier (and extract with no heat, as their name says) but give the highest juice yield with the most nutrients.

- **Rice cooker:** Looking for fluffy, perfectly cooked grains with the flick of a switch? A 5-cup model is great for a family of four, but a 3-cup is best for smaller households. Again, pick one that's easy to clean and has large and accessible buttons; avoid those with too many extra doodads.

The Little Things

These are the oft-reached-for tools that sit proudly in a crock, stoveside, or are nestled in the drawer nearest our prep station. As a general rule, simpler tends to be better with these essential friends. We generally steer clear of single-use tools—but everyone's got their favorite gadgets. If you use it and love it, keep it. (Psst: Check out Your Kitchen Cheat Sheet on page 148 for any measurement conversions you may need.)

Must-Haves

- **Box grater:** Look for one with a no-slip base, an easily grippable handle, and a sharp stainless-steel grating surface on each of its four to six distinct sides. It should tackle the hard (potatoes) and the soft (mozzarella) equally well.

- **Can opener:** We like a basic model (no magnets or special tricks) with a large turning knob and ergonomic handles.

- **Colander:** Smaller holes make it as good for draining grains and pasta as for washing vegetables. Plastic and metal versions both work great.

- **Dry measuring cups:** Whether made of metal or plastic, pick a set with ¼ cup, ⅓ cup, ½ cup, and 1 cup measures.

- **Fish spatula:** Typically made of stainless steel, its thin edge slides under lots more than fish—delicate fried eggs, tender all-beef patties, cheesy fritters, and more.

- **Kitchen towels:** We're faithful to large, lint-free, quick-drying cotton flour-sack towels. A couple of thicker, extra-absorbent utility towels round out the pack.

- **Ladle:** Get a roomy one made of stainless steel, and soup's on. (Rum punch, too!)

- **Liquid measuring cups:** One 4-cup measure and one 1-cup measure are all you need. We like ones made of glass.

- **Measuring spoons:** Decorative sets are cute, but not as accurate as classic stainless-steel or plastic spoons.

- **Mixing and prep bowls:** A stainless-steel or glass nesting set of three is all you'll need for prepping, mixing, and serving.

- **Peeler:** We'll happily use a straight or Y-shaped peeler with a plastic or stainless-steel handle, as long as it feels good to hold and the blade is sturdy and sharp.

- **Pepper mill:** We prefer fresh-ground pepper over preground any day of the week! Pick whatever design you like best but make sure it's easy to refill.

- **Rasp-style grater:** You might know this as a Microplane. We love it for finely zesting citrus, grating garlic to a paste, and piling fluffy banks of Parmesan on pasta.

- **Silicone spatulas:** Get one large and one small, ideally without a detachable head (which can come apart easily and trap bits of food and bacteria inside).

- **Spider or slotted spoon:** For lifting just-boiled eggs and crisp-fried falafel from the pot, you can't go wrong with a metal variety, which won't melt—unlike the plastic versions.

CONTINUED

- **Tongs:** For turning steaks and tossing greens, look for a stainless-steel set with a strong, steady grip. A collapsing and locking feature allows for convenient storage, but isn't a "must."

- **Wooden spoons:** We'd be lost without at least two, one with a bowl for tasting and one with a flat edge for scraping.

Nice-to-Haves

- **¼-cup liquid measure:** For the precision-minded, a glass mini measuring cup delineates tablespoons, teaspoons, and ounces.

- **Apron:** It's got us covered in the kitchen.

- **Citrus reamer:** The perfect tool for getting every last drop of juice. We like the simple wooden style.

- **Corkscrew:** For bottles of red and white, we prefer simple folding "waiter's friend" models over the ones with "arms."

- **Digital scale:** For super-exact measuring in your cooking and baking.

- **Fine-mesh sieve:** This strainer produces silky-smooth purées and sauces.

- **Funnel:** A thin-mouthed one is great for decanting olive oil from jug to cruet (see "oil cruet" entry), and a wide-mouthed model can help dried goods go easily into jars. Stainless-steel or plastic types both work great.

- **Instant-read thermometer:** With this helpful tool, you'll never undercook meat or bread again. Though thermometers can range quite a bit in cost and quality, we prefer an inexpensive to middle-of-the-road model. What matters most is a quick and accurate temperature measure (3 to 5 seconds), sturdy build, long probe length, and an easy-to-read dial.

- **Kitchen twine:** Get a ball (food-grade or made of 100 percent cotton) for tying roasts and making herb bundles.

- **Mandoline:** Spring for a thin, flat, Japanese-style model with a sharp stainless-steel blade and a hand guard. (Watch your fingers!)

- **Mini offset spatula:** A cookie-lifting, mayo-spreading, and cake-frosting dynamo made of stainless steel.

- **Oil cruet:** This dispenser is easier to hold and maneuver than a giant can of olive oil. There are handsome options made of dark glass or stoneware.

- **Pastry brush:** The old-school version—an actual wooden-handled paintbrush—does the job beautifully. Silicone models with an attached head are good options, too, especially for basting barbecued meats with glaze and brushing egg wash onto delicate pastries.

- **Pot holders:** We love these for handling hot pots or doubling as a trivet, but folded (and bone-dry!) dish towels are easy, always-in-reach substitutes.

- **Rolling pin:** Not just for pies, rolling pins are great for tenderizing meat or crushing graham crackers. Lightweight, easy-to-clean wood is the way to go.

- **Ruler:** Sure, we can eyeball with the best of 'em—but knowing for sure means getting just the right thickness on a rolled-out crust (soggy bottoms no more!).

- **Salt cellar:** Choose something on the bigger side, so you're not always topping it off.

- **Whisk:** Stainless-steel or silicone balloon whisks are your best bet. But unless you whip a lot of cream or egg whites, you can get by with a fork just fine.

Equipment Swaps:
How to MacGyver Your Way to a Meal

You've gotten excited about a new recipe and then realized that—drat!—you don't have the necessary tools. But it's no reason to give up! See if you can get the job done with what you have.

No apron? A clean kitchen towel tucked around the waist is a fine stand-in.

No citrus reamer? Twist the tines of a fork into a halved fruit's flesh, and squeeze.

No fine-mesh sieve? Layer a thin, clean kitchen towel over a colander to strain.

No food processor? Use your blender. Most blenders can handle a pesto or purée—but a blender can't chop things up. For that, try using a rolling pin to bash cookies or nuts to crumbs in a ziplock or silicone bag.

No pastry brush? Distribute an egg wash or glaze with your best tools: hands.

No potato masher? Grab a whisk and mash away at those creamy potatoes.

No rolling pin? Track down a wine bottle (just give it a quick rinse beforehand).

No sifter? Add your ingredients to a fine-mesh sieve and shake the sieve to sift.

No stand or handheld electric mixer? For a simple creaming of sugar into butter, a wooden spoon and some elbow grease make a good sub.

The Tools Our
Test Kitchen Can't
Cook Without

Josh Cohen is Food52's former test kitchen director and our current chef-in-residence. For years, he was in charge of the food for our in-house photo shoots, and responsible for managing our test kitchen's always-full fridge and pantry (among other things). We asked him about the tools he reaches for most.

Q What are your most-used (and most-beloved) kitchen prep tools?

A A sharp 8-inch chef's knife is the first tool I grab every day at work. Besides that, I use a wooden spoon, rubber spatula, Microplane, tongs, Y-shaped vegetable peeler, and fish spatula. But my best-loved items are all related to pasta: a hand-crank roller I've owned for more than 10 years, a chitarra for cutting long strands, and a gnocchi board for creating those little ridges.

Q What can't you imagine cooking without?

A A large cutting board. I hate trying to chop something on a small board because food ends up falling off the board and onto the floor. I also like to have a large stockpot or Dutch oven and a large skillet (overcrowding a pan is a no-go). My favorite item, by far, is a cast-iron skillet by the maker Smithey. It's a heavy-duty pan for searing, and it also becomes nonstick the more you use it and take care of it.

Q Which small prep tool has been the biggest game changer for you?

A A mini offset spatula is always useful to have. For any recipe that requires some finesse—from smoothing a batter to working with frosting—it's my very best friend.

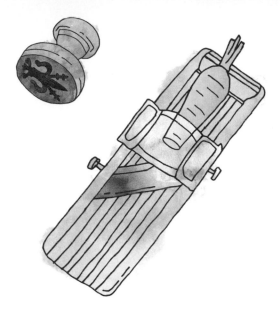

Q What was your first kitchen-related investment piece?

A An 8-inch chef's knife and a whetstone. A good stone is important to maintaining your blade. And I would've bought a high-speed blender, but my wife already had a Vitamix blender when we started dating—that was a huge windfall!

Q Do you have a soft spot for any single-use kitchen gadgets?

A Nope. I have a Japanese mandoline that I love, and a mortar and pestle that isn't totally necessary, but I like it. I try to be a minimalist.

Q What's on your kitchen wish list?

A I am very happy—I have most everything I need. Although, I guess it would be fun to own a corzetti stamp (more pasta tools!).

Q What's your favorite spot to shop for tools?

A Chef supplier JB Prince is a great store.

Pots & Pans: Our Bread & Butter

You don't need a lot of pots and pans to get the job done, but having a range of shapes and sizes opens the door to a world of new recipes. These are the ones we reach for on the daily. (Psst: Check out Your Kitchen Cheat Sheet on page 148 for any measurement conversions you may need.)

Must-Haves

- **2- and 4-quart lidded saucepans:** You'll want one of each size. Look for a heavy version to help avoid scorching, with a comfortable, long handle that conducts very little concentrated heat and remains cooler on the stove. We like stainless steel or carbon steel.

- **5- to 7-quart Dutch oven:** This is your soup pot, braise pot, bean pot, and bread oven. Pick a heavyweight enameled one with a light-colored interior (to see what's going on in there as you cook) and a pretty outer color (so you can serve straight from it).

- **8-quart lidded stockpot:** Break this out for pasta night and to make chicken broth. You only need one, so make sure it's a hefty, strong-bottomed stainless-steel model with a well-fitting lid.

- **8- and 10-inch frying pans:** Buy one of each for all your searing, sizzling, and frying needs. Stainless steel or carbon steel work best—but at least one should be nonstick (see page 19). A well-fitting lid's a nice-to-have.

- **10- to 12-inch cast-iron skillet:** We can barely imagine cooking without one. Take care of it well for a nearly nonstick surface (see page 18 to learn how).

Nice-to-Haves

- **½- to 1-quart butter warmer:** For boiling two eggs, warming milk for cocoa, or, ahem, melting a stick of butter, choose an enameled or stainless-steel pot with a lid.

- **1½-quart rice pot:** It's designed to cook rice perfectly, but it can make lots of other stove-top cameos (like poaching eggs or making oatmeal for two). Enamel is our preference, and lidded.

- **14-inch wok:** Carbon steel can get screaming hot and is naturally nonstick. This roomy size gives you plenty of space to stir-fry your heart out.

- **Casserole dish:** You'll want one of these in oven-safe stoneware if you love baked mac and cheese or apple crisp. A pretty one you can serve in is a big plus.

- **Griddle/grill pan:** Pick a carbon-steel or cast-iron model that lies directly over your stove's burners. A reversible pan—with a smooth griddle on one side and grill pan grates on the other—is even better for smaller kitchens. Enjoy those burgers!

- **Roasting pan:** Stainless steel is nearly indestructible, but enamel-coated is easiest to clean. A model with an insert rack is a nice-to-have, especially if you're in charge of this year's Thanksgiving turkey.

- **Steamer:** For steaming vegetables, dumplings, and tender fish fillets galore, choose a folding stainless-steel or rigid bamboo version, equally good in our book.

How to Take a Cast-Iron Pan from Rusty to Ready (& Keep It That Way)

Cast-iron pans aren't just ultra-utilitarian—often passed down from cook to cook, they're storytellers, too. They've got an unfair reputation for being high maintenance, but, really, cooking with a cast-iron pan is like keeping a guitar in tune: Give it a little attention here and there, and it sings. No matter in what condition your pan comes to you, it can likely be salvaged with these simple steps. Repeat them whenever it's looking lackluster.

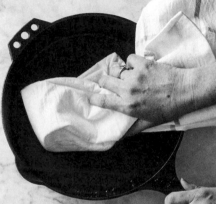

1. Heat the oven to 400°F. Sprinkle your pan generously with coarse salt (like kosher) and then use a halved potato, cut-side down, to scrub the salt all over. The salt will start to look pretty gross.

2. Rinse with water and dry well.

3. Swirl a few teaspoons of neutral oil (like canola) all around the pan to form a very thin coating, and pop the pan into the hot oven for an hour.

4. Carefully remove the pan from the oven and wipe out any remaining oil. You're ready to cook!

Nonstick Pans: The Good, the Bad, the Ugly

Nonstick pans . . . rock! We love using them to make crispy fried rice, sear chicken breasts—you name it. But they're worth researching because many of them get their nonstickiness from harsh chemicals. Track down a pan that is **naturally nonstick** (like ceramic-coated or carbon steel) or otherwise **free of PFA, PFOA, and PFTE** (aka Teflon, a chemical often found in nonstick cookware). When you find a type you like, get two of them; use them both with nonmetal utensils, and wash gently. Avoid nonstick bakeware, most of which hasn't yet gotten the nontoxic treatment.

And if your nonstick pan ever peels, flakes, or scratches, *toss it*— you don't want that stuff in your beautiful sunny-side-up eggs.

Bakeware: Oven & Out

Baking may require some special tools, but having just a *few* of them in your kitchen will totally change your game: special-occasion cakes, morning muffins, and gooey-in-the-middle cookies can all be yours. Our baking's all the better with these essentials. (Psst: Check out Your Kitchen Cheat Sheet on page 148 for any measurement conversions you may need.)

Must-Haves

- **9 by 13-inch baking pan:** Glass, ceramic, or metal (aluminum or stainless steel) all function the same—your call! Fruit buckles, enchiladas, and baked pastas all fit well in here.

- **Loaf pans:** For banana bread and meat loaf alike, you'll want two matching 8 by 4-inch or 9 by 5-inch aluminum or stainless-steel pans; recipes often yield two loaves.

- **Muffin tin:** We recommend aluminum or stainless steel but not nonstick (that's what muffin liners or just a good greasing is for). Pick one with a dozen cups.

- **Oven thermometer:** This is a $5 tool for better, more accurate baking. Its tight-fitting hinges or hooks clip onto an oven rack and stay put.

- **Parchment paper:** Use it for lining pans, wrapping treats for friends, and catching drips when you glaze a cake. Frankly, we couldn't bake without it.

- **Rimmed sheet pans:** Stock at least two of these in stainless steel or aluminum. "Half sheets" (18 by 13 inches) are our most-reached-for size to roast veggies, bake snickerdoodles, and corral ingredients into place before starting a recipe. "Quarter sheets" (9 by 13 inches) are great for smaller jobs, like roasting a handful of walnuts.

- **Round cake pans:** Stock two aluminum or stainless-steel pans 9 inches in diameter and 2 inches deep, and you're on your way to many a layer cake.

- **Spring-loaded scooper:** These come in a range of sizes and easily scoop rounds of cookie dough, meatball mix, or perfectly portioned muffin batter.

- **Square cake pan:** Look for an 8-inch or 9-inch pan in aluminum, stainless steel, or glass that's at least 2 inches deep. Lemon bars, blondies, and cheesy cornbread have a happy home here.

- **Wire cooling rack:** The more air that can circulate around your baked goods, the more evenly they'll cool—and the sooner you can tear into them.

Nice-to-Haves

- **9-inch pie plate:** A no-frills glass pie dish (the better to see the bottom of the pie!) is the most versatile.

- **9- to 10-inch springform pan:** For cheesecakes and anything else that needs a high-sided pan, aluminum or stainless-steel versions are the way to go.

- **10- to 12-cup Bundt pan:** For all of your old-school coffee-cake needs, choose a classic Bundt in either aluminum or stainless steel.

- **Bench scraper:** Use it to scrape bits of ingredients from the counter or a mixing bowl, cut dough into pieces, or transfer chopped vegetables from cutting board to pan. We like it in stainless steel or plastic.

- **Cookie cutters:** Strong, sharp, stainless-steel cutters will give you a clean slice. A set of graduated round cutters (straight or fluted) goes a long way.

- **Silicone sheet-pan liner:** Sure, it's pricier than parchment paper, but you'll have it forever.

Tableware: Your Dinner's Handsome Canvas

As with all kitchen tools, we consider beauty *and* functionality when it comes to tableware. These items should be nice to look at but **easily stackable**, **not too fragile**, and most often **dishwasher- and microwave-safe**. Our shelves are filled with a mix of vintage china, new box-store models, and handmade beauties from ceramicists we love. We prefer fun mismatching sets, too, but in a streamlined palette to tie it all together. (Psst: Check out Your Kitchen Cheat Sheet on page 148 for any measurement conversions you may need.)

For Everyday Eating

- **Big plates:** We're talking dinner-size (10 to 12 inches in diameter).

- **Small plates:** For apps, snacks, you name it (we like ones from 4 to 7 inches).

- **Big bowls:** For stews, hearty salads, and more. You might also consider the ever-handy "blate," aka a low, wide bowl.

- **Small bowls:** Cereal, soup, and dips have a place in these.

- **Teensy bowls:** For olives and their pits or a handful of bar nuts—the cuter the better! Stock as many as you want.

- **Tall glasses:** For water and highballs.

- **Short glasses:** For OJ with breakfast and wine at dinnertime.

- **Mugs:** Mugs are superpersonal (weird but true!). Don't let us cramp your style.

- **Utensils:** Must be dishwasher-safe and nice to hold. Steak knives are great if you eat steak regularly, and you can also use them for chicken, burgers, and even thickly cut cauliflower or eggplant. (We keep one or two of these per person.)

- **Cloth napkins:** They save paper and help set the scene.

For Parties & Crowds

- **Cake stand:** For putting your cake/pie/fruit bowl on a pedestal.

- **Large serving bowls:** Two will cover your pasta night and weekly fruit haul. We love ones in ceramic and wood.

- **Large serving utensils:** You'll need just two serving spoons to dish up the goods at your dinner party, one slotted and one solid; also, a large serving fork.

- **Pitcher:** When it isn't serving up drinks, it doubles as a vase.

- **Platters:** Two is a good place to start. Get a mix of shapes and sizes, but make sure they're heatproof (so you can keep plated food warm until you're ready to serve) and easy to clean (nothing overly bulky, heavy, or ornate, please).

- **Serving board:** To carve a turkey or build a killer charcuterie or cheese plate. (You can also use a big wooden cutting board for this.)

- **Tablecloths:** One in a light neutral, and another in a dark and dramatic hue.

- **Trays:** For breakfast in bed or creating a mini moveable bar, two standard trays—one medium and one large—are all you need.

A Field Guide to Food-Storage Containers

Whether you're looking to save the last spoonfuls of Thanksgiving stuffing or house a week's worth of roasted vegetables, you'll need a collection of durable, versatile storage containers. We look for ones with the following features:

- Made of **clear glass,** so you can peek at what's inside, and forever bid farewell to smells and stains; **clear heavy-duty plastic,** which is featherlight, basically unbreakable, and easy to tote around; or **food-safe stainless steel,** which isn't see-through or microwave-safe, but is dishwasher-safe, durable, and eco-friendly.

- **Spill-proof, dishwasher-safe, and microwave-safe;** it's simply practical.

- **Stackable bases with stackable lids** to help avoid haphazard storage.

- **A variety of sizes** for corralling your week's meal prep.

Must-Haves

(Here's a starter kit for a household of two; and check out Your Kitchen Cheat Sheet on page 148 for any measurement conversions you may need.)

- **Large containers (2 to 3):** Choose 6- to 7-cup sizes for large amounts of leftovers.

- **Medium containers (5 to 7):** These are the 2- to 4-cup containers for packing lunches, stashing smallish amounts of leftovers, and keeping meal-prep components in line.

- **Small containers (2 to 3):** Little 1-cup bowls for the odd half-avocado or lemon, a batch of dip, or your morning yogurt.

- **Insulated thermos mug or bottle:** One per person for coffee and tea on the go.

- **Reusable water bottle:** One per person for water sipping. Stainless steel is the most durable, but we like glass bottles, too.

Nice-to-Haves

- **10- to 16-ounce insulated wide-mouth Thermos:** Use for transporting (and keeping warm) soup, oatmeal, or your favorite stewy stroganoff.

- **Bento- or tiffin-style lunchbox:** Their nifty compartments are a cinch to clean and keep wet foods separate from dry.

- **Very small containers:** Pick anything between 1 ounce and ½ cup for salad dressing and to-go snacks.

Unnecessary-but-Lovable Unitaskers

- **Ceramic butter keeper:** Once you've slathered perfectly spreadable butter on a crusty loaf, you'll know why we swear by these little friends.

- **Cheese vault:** Your cave-aged Gouda will stay funky and fresh. Look for a food-grade silicone model with an adjustable compartment size.

- **Wooden, melamine, or steel bread box:** It keeps your loaves crisp-crusted and out of the way.

For Adding Some Comfy & Cozy

A kitchen needs to withstand some serious wear and tear—
but that doesn't mean *everything* has to be stainless steel
and silicone. The delight is in the details, the not-necessarily-
functional things that make a kitchen *your* kitchen. If walking
into the kitchen makes you smile, you'll want to spend more
time in there.

Here Are a Few Ideas:

- Taped-up love notes
- A big vase of flowers to greet you
- A cheerful rug to stand on
- Hand-me-down tools, treasures, and
  recipe cards from the people who've
  cooked for you
- Photos of the people for whom you
  most like to cook
- Hook-hung vintage copper pots

A family of collected trinkets—
like quirky wooden spoons

A bright lamp (floor, table, or wall-hung, depending on your space) to browse your very favorite cookbooks

Potted or hanging plants

Art of all kinds

Funny flea-market knickknacks, like a parade of miniature animal figurines

A radio or speakers to tune into while you cook

Paring Back: How to Know
When Your Tools Have to Go

Okay, so you've gotten the lay of the land, and you're filling up and settling into your kitchen. But if you're anything like us, how and what you cook will change all the time, and so will your tools. It's worth asking yourself these questions every few months.

- **What have I used—or not used—in the past year?** If you haven't picked up that tool recently, it might be worth donating. Our exception: the "big feast" items that you pull out every now and then for holidays and dinner parties.

- **What are my unnecessary duplicates?** Unless otherwise noted in this chapter, you really only need one of each kitchen tool. So, next time you unearth your growing collection of Y-peelers, set your favorite one aside. Put the still-functional duplicate items in a bag to donate to a charity or to a friend starting their own kitchen.

- **What unitaskers can be replaced with a sharp knife or kitchen shears?** Unless you use them often, chances are you don't *need* that pizza cutter or ravioli roller, pretty as they might be. Consider sticking with the knife instead.

- **What's out of shape?** Dull-edged knives, sticky pans—these are the things that need 15 minutes of your (or a specialist's) attention. If they're truly broken or will cost more to fix than to replace, it's probably time to clear them out.

- **What's looking especially dated?** These may be the things you use quite often but haven't turned a critical eye to in a while. If they're more than a little banged up or are operating less than perfectly, it might be time to upgrade. (Bonus: More modern tools and appliances are usually slimmer, not to mention more energy efficient.)

- **What kitchen tools make me smile?** Of course, the preceding rules are just guidelines—if your two spice grinders are continually getting use *and* delighting you, go ahead and keep them both.

The Big Stock-Up: Our Tips for Shopping, Sourcing & Investing

Selecting a kitchen's trappings is a careful dance: You'll want to prioritize the tools that work well and reliably, are pleasing to use, and that won't break the bank. Our favorite approach is to shop around at a mix of specialty kitchen stores (for beloved name brands), restaurant supply stores (for inexpensive, workaday basics), thrift stores (for secondhand greats), and more.

For more ideas about what to buy, head to the Sourcebook on page 146.

- **Specialty kitchen stores (in person or online):** Our favorite sources for quality kitchenware include **OXO** for small hand tools; **KitchenAid**, **Cuisinart**, and **Breville** for appliances, like mixers and food processors; **Staub** and **Le Creuset** for enameled pans and Dutch ovens; **Smithey** and **Lodge** for cast iron; **GreenPan** and **Ballarini** for nonstick pans; and **Zwilling** (specifically Demeyere) and **All-Clad** for 5-ply stainless-steel cookware. We also love **Crate & Barrel** and **CB2** for tableware.

- **Restaurant supply stores:** This is the place to stock up on sheet pans, thermometers, rolling pins, mixing bowls, some cookware (like woks), tongs, measuring cups and spoons, wooden spoons, and even knives. The equipment will be hardworking, frill-less, and inexpensive.

- **Thrift stores:** Your local thrift store's kitchen section is a treasure trove. You'll find glass and metal baking pans galore, cast iron of all kinds, glass measuring cups, gently used appliances, and vintage dishware, flatware, and servingware aplenty—as well as Bundt pans. Thrift stores are rich in Bundt pans!

- **IKEA:** Yep—our Swedish big-box friend gets a shout-out of its own. We'd be remiss not to sing the praises of IKEA's basic kitchen towels (not even a dollar a pop!), plastic cutting boards, and affordable bamboo butcher blocks.

The Affordable Kitchen: Basics on a Budget

Buying tools for a kitchen can feel overwhelming, especially if you're looking to save some money. But a small investment can go far—*really* far! Here's a shopping list of our desert-island kitchen essentials, all for just a couple hundred bucks. Some guidelines: Shop at restaurant supply stores over specialty home and cooking stores, buy generic-brand tools, and compare prices of individual items versus prepackaged sets (sometimes, for example, three single mixing bowls can cost less than a nesting trio). Hit the thrift store or yard sales for perfectly good, preloved tools, and we bet you could do it even more affordably!

For the rest of our tool recommendations, head to page 146 (and check out Your Kitchen Cheat Sheet on page 148 for any measurement conversions you may need).

- **1-cup glass liquid measure** for broths, marinades, and beyond.

- **3- to 5-quart aluminum-clad stainless-steel pot** or saucepan with lid for boiling eggs and cooking rice.

- **8- to 12-quart aluminum-clad stainless-steel pot** with lid for making soup and pasta and so much more.

- **8- to 10-inch cast-iron pan** for frying eggs and baking cornbread.

- **Aluminum rimmed half-sheet pan** for roasting vegetables and baking batches of cookies.

- **Chef's knife** for leading the way.

- **Large plastic cutting board** to do all your chopping on (as big as you can find).

- **Medium- or fine-mesh stainless-steel or aluminum strainer** for catching everything.

- **Silicone spatula** for getting every last drop.

- **Stainless-steel or glass mixing bowls** for mixing and serving (set of three).

- **Stainless-steel fish spatula** for flipping burgers and lifting pancakes.

- **Stainless-steel measuring spoons** for confident baking and seasoning.

- **Stainless-steel or plastic measuring cups** for flour, grains, and beans.

- **Wooden spoon** for stirring and stirring.

The Dreamboat Investments

With ingredients and tools, we try to buy the best we can afford. But there are some tools we can buy cheaply and cheerfully without sacrificing functionality, and others where craftsmanship, durability, and environmental concerns are worth extra consideration. For the later, shopping in a slightly higher price bracket changes the game entirely. If you can invest up to a few hundred dollars on each, these are the tools that are worth it.

- **Extra-large cutting board or butcher block:** What's the truest luxury in the kitchen? Room to spread out! A large, solid-wood cutting board is a worthwhile buy. John Boos makes near-indestructible ones in a variety of sizes; their boards that are 12 by 18 inches and 1½ inches thick start at about $70.

- **Handheld electric or stand mixer:** If you love to bake, it's hard to imagine going without one of these. Be sure to consider professionally refurbished models, which are good as new and much less expensive. You can find these online, either from the manufacturers themselves, electronics stores, or major online retailers; alternatively, look for secondhand items at thrift stores and yard sales. We love the classic KitchenAid mixers: new 7-speed handheld models are under $100; refurbished 5-quart stand mixers start at about $200; and new stand-mixer models range between $250 and $500.

- **Heavy enameled Dutch oven:** Thick-walled, heat-retaining, beautiful, and all-purpose, you'll use this pot forever. A 6-quart Lodge pot starts at about $60; a Staub of the same size starts at about $200; a Le Creuset version goes for about $350. Be sure to keep an eye out for the occasional sale on these, as the discounts can be big.

- **High-powered blenders:** These hefty machines help us make all things smooth and silky—soups, smoothies, sauces, and the creamiest cashew cheese. Look for these refurbished, too, or at your neighborhood yard sale. At these places, you can even get 'em for about $200.

- **Knives:** If $35 can get you a good knife and $50 can get you a great one, $100 to $150 will buy you a truly excellent one. Our test kitchen favors those from Zwilling J. A. Henckels, Opinel, and Miyabi.

- **Nontoxic nonstick pans:** Nonstick pans aren't terribly expensive, but it's worth it to spend more on models free of certain chemicals (see page 19 for more on this). GreenPan and Ballarini both make beautiful, reliable ones—and you should be able to get a set of two for under $100.

Our Resident Genius
KRISTEN MIGLORE'S
Kitchen Kit

Kristen Miglore is Food52's Genius Recipes excavator. She's unearthed some of the most cherished dishes of our time from many a brilliant chef: the game-changers we know by heart. Kristen's neat kitchen is where she cooks through them all. In addition to her must-have tools, it features potted plants, charming knickknacks, and favorite cookbooks in a hidden nook, so it's always a place Kristen loves to be. Have a look-see into where she makes magic.

→ I've always wanted Genius Recipes to be welcoming to all home cooks, so the recipes call for pretty minimal, basic equipment. I, myself, rely most on a big (but thin and lightweight) **santoku knife**.

→ I cull my less-used tools regularly but do **keep multiples of ones I use on repeat** in a single cooking session (like kitchen shears, silicone spatulas, whisks, and wooden spoons), so I don't have to wash them in between.

→ The things I can't cook without are a **podcast** and a **decent speaker**. (Putting my phone in a restaurant-supply quart container works as a sound-amplifying hack.)

→ In my future dream kitchen, I hope to have a **permanent island with a stove-top**. For now, I've settled for a **basic stainless-steel table** from a restaurant supply store, where I can prep ingredients up top and house pots and pans below.

Recipe testing has forced me to be extra efficient with my space, storage, and (obsessive) cleanup habits to minimize chaos.

CHAPTER 2

Stocking Up

In this chapter, we'll walk you through our *whats*, *hows*, and *whys* for stocking the pantry and the fridge, the standbys that guide us through our weeknight dinners and on-a-whim cooking adventures, plus tips for shopping and sourcing. (We've got a few ideas for pantry dinners up our sleeves, too.) We bet you'll share a couple of our essentials, but we also expect you to have your own to add—so take this guide and run absolutely wild with it.

6 Super-Simple Steps to Stock Your Pantry

You know what's a common misconception? That the pantry is a storage closet, a place to stockpile teetering towers of boxes and bottles. Not very inspiring! A pantry that makes us want to sing with joy is one that's thoughtfully stocked with a mix of versatile staples. And it starts with these guidelines.

1. **Buy only what you need.** For the next month or two, that is. This way, you'll avoid food waste, your pantry will be less overwhelmed, and you'll be able to redirect funds from quantity to quality.

2. **But go ahead and grab canned and bottled staples in bulk.** If you have the space, save money by buying staples you'll go through quickly, like canned tomatoes or beans, by the flat. (You may also want to snatch up multiples of any on-sale favorites or specialty ingredients that are hard to come by.)

3. **Invest in what you use every day.** You can really taste the difference in highest-quality olive oil, vinegar, and spices, so seek out the best you can afford and your dinner will thank you. (See page 59 for the things we budget a little more for.)

4. **Shop around.** Buy from suppliers you trust or stores you know have a high turnover rate. You might have different favorite stores for amazing bulk bins (see page 40 for more on this), spices, and specialty items. For the rest, your local supermarket, wholesale club, or online retailer is just the place.

5. **Bring your own bags and/or jars to the bulk bins when you can.** It cuts down on plastic-bag waste, lets you buy exactly the amount you want, and makes it easier to . . .

6. **Decant!** A set of jars or airtight canisters doesn't just look good, it's also more space-efficient, makes it easier to find what you need, and keeps food fresher. (Page 25 has the lowdown on the best containers to use.)

Pantry Friends for Reliable, Delicious Dinners (& Lunches)

Okay, now you know *how* to stock, but what kind of stuff should you buy? First, think about the dishes you like to cook and then make a list. Channeling Kerala? You'll want ghee, black mustard seeds, and cumin. If you're mastering the art of French cooking, herbes de Provence and shallots are musts. If you're vegan, swap honey for maple syrup and load up on the nutritional yeast.

Here, you'll find our tried-and-true faves in two sections: **The Short List**, a set of ingredients so useful and versatile, we think everyone should have them in their pantry; and **The Long List**, which is like the "extended cut" version of your favorite album—a great place to start when you're looking to expand your pantry toolbox. Feel free to tailor these lists so they ring true for you.

The Short List

Cans, Bottles, Boxes & Jars

BUILDING BLOCKS

- Anchovies (packed in oil)
- Boxed low-sodium chicken or vegetable stock
- Canned beans (like garbanzo, black, or cannellini)
- Canned or jarred tuna
- Canned whole plum tomatoes

CONDIMENTS, SAUCES & PERSONALITY-PACKED PALS

- Capers
- Cornichons or other pickles
- Dijon mustard
- Hot sauce
- Ketchup
- Mayonnaise
- Peanut (or another nut) butter

- Soy sauce or tamari
- Tomato paste

OILS & VINEGARS

- Extra-virgin olive oil (an affordable one for cooking; an extra-special one for drizzling)
- Neutral oil (like safflower, vegetable, or canola)
- Versatile vinegars (like red wine, white wine, or apple cider)

SWEET STUFF

- Honey, maple syrup, and/or agave syrup
- Jam

Dry Goods

BAKING

- All-purpose flour
- Baking powder

CONTINUED

- Baking soda
- Brown sugar (light and/or dark)
- Chocolate bars or chips for baking
- Cornstarch
- Granulated white sugar
- Vanilla extract

HERBS & SPICES

- Bay leaves (dried)
- Black peppercorns
- Cayenne (ground)
- Chili powder (salt-free)
- Cinnamon (ground)
- Cloves (ground)
- Coriander (whole seeds or ground)
- Cumin (whole seeds or ground)
- Curry powder
- Ginger (ground)
- Kosher and/or fine sea salt
- Nutmeg (whole)
- Oregano (dried)
- Thyme (dried)
- Turmeric (ground)
- Red pepper flakes
- Smoked paprika (ground)

NUTS, FRUIT & OTHER DRIED ODDS & ENDS

- Coffee (whole bean) and/or tea (bags or leaves)
- Dried fruit to cook with and snack on (like raisins or dates)
- Nuts and/or seeds to cook with and snack on (like almonds or sunflower seeds)

PRODUCE

- Garlic
- Onions and/or shallots

STARCHY STANDBYS

- Bread crumbs (plain or panko)
- Bread for slicing
- Dried lentils (sturdy green, brown, or black; varieties that get soft and stewy, like red or yellow)
- Dried pasta (long shapes, like spaghetti; short ones, like penne)
- Grains (like quinoa, farro, wheatberries, or freekeh)
- Old-fashioned oats
- White or brown rice

WHERE, OH WHERE, ARE THE BULK BINS?

There are lots of benefits to buying from bulk bins: You can get exactly the amount you want and bring your own reusable containers to fill, and the bins have high turnover, meaning the food will be fresh. And while bulk bins are most used for dry goods, some shops have dispensers for liquids, like honey, tahini, and even laundry detergent. You can most reliably find bulk bins at health food stores and food co-ops; you might also check grocery stores (like Whole Foods) and specialty markets (like Middle Eastern grocers). Litterless.com is a helpful online resource with guides to shopping bulk bins in every state in the United States.

The Long List

Cans, Bottles, Boxes & Jars

BUILDING BLOCKS

- Chipotles en adobo (canned)
- Full-fat coconut milk (canned)
- Tahini

CONDIMENTS, SAUCES & PERSONALITY-PACKED PALS

- Hoisin sauce
- Thai curry paste (red or green)
- Worcestershire sauce

OILS & VINEGARS

- Aged balsamic vinegar
- Coconut oil (unrefined)
- Mirin
- Red and/or white wines for cooking (dry)
- Sesame oil (toasted)
- Sherry vinegar

SWEET STUFF

- Molasses
- Pomegranate molasses

Dry Goods

BAKING

- Almond extract
- Cocoa powder
- Confectioners' sugar
- Whole-wheat flour

HERBS & SPICES

- Black mustard seeds
- Cardamom (whole pods or ground)
- Chile flakes (like Aleppo, Maras, or gochugaru)
- Chile powder (single-variety, like chipotle)
- Fennel seeds (whole seeds)
- Five-spice powder
- Flaky sea salt (like Maldon)
- Garam masala
- Nutritional yeast
- Sesame seeds (white or black)
- Star anise (whole pods)
- Sumac (ground)
- White peppercorns
- Za'atar

NUTS, FRUIT & OTHER DRIED ODDS & ENDS

- Coconut (unsweetened, shredded, or flaked)
- Dried shiitake mushrooms
- Konbu
- Nori
- Sun-dried tomatoes

PRODUCE

- White and/or sweet potatoes

STARCHY STANDBYS

- Cornmeal (medium-grind)
- Dried beans (like garbanzo, black turtle, cannellini, or black-eyed peas)
- Rice noodles
- Short-grain rice (like arborio or Japanese)
- Soba noodles

How Long Can You Keep Pantry Stuff, Anyway?

As comforting as it might be to have a stockpile big enough to last you a decade, nonperishables actually do have best-by dates, before which they'll taste their best and have the most nutrients. We've got some tips for prolonging the life of your pantry goods—and a handy use-by schedule to follow at home.

- **Keep 'em cool, dark, and dry.** These are three beautiful words when it comes to pantries, whose contents can be sensitive to light, heat, and damp.

- **Airtight containers are a must.** Not only do they allow you to keep your nuts, grains, and such for even longer, they also discourage unwanted pests. You only have to have one visit from pantry moths to know just how invaluable airtight storage is. (Have we convinced you yet?)

UP TO 3 MONTHS

Nut flours

Whole-grain flours

UP TO 6 MONTHS

Baking powder   Chocolate bars

Baking soda   Whole-grain rice

Bread crumbs

UP TO 9 MONTHS

White flour

UP TO 1 YEAR	**UP TO 18 MONTHS**	**UP TO 2 YEARS**		**THESE LAST A LOOONG TIME!**	
Nut or seed oils	Olive oil [1]	Canned or jarred goods	Dried pasta	Brown sugar [2]	Salt
Spices		Chocolate chips	Vegetable/ neutral oils	Cornstarch	Vanilla extract
		Dried beans and lentils		Honey [3]	Vinegar
				Milled rice	White sugar

1. Unopened; once open, you've got 6 months.

2. If it ever gets hard, just stick a slice of soft bread in its container, seal, and then store for a day or two. And voilà—soft, scoopable sugar.

3. If it crystallizes, it's still totally safe to eat—just heat it up for 10 seconds in the microwave.

How to Make Soup from a Stone:
Pantry-Based Mini-Recipes for Dinner

We're huge fans of pantry meals—nothing leaves us more triumphant than making a feast that skirts an extra trip to the store. Here are our favorite ways to do just that with a few canned staples. (And for a refresher on cooking basics, head to Chapter 4).

Canned Tomatoes

Tomatoey White Bean Stew

In a shallow saucepan over medium-low heat, soften 3 sliced garlic cloves with a pinch of red pepper flakes in a splash of extra-virgin olive oil. Add 1 bunch stemmed and torn kale plus two 28-ounce cans whole peeled tomatoes, crushed. Simmer until thickened, 10 minutes, then add a drained 15-ounce can of white beans and heat fully. Season with kosher salt and grated Parm.

Shakshuka

Thinly slice 1 onion, 1 bell pepper, and 2 garlic cloves. Add to a skillet over medium-high heat and soften in a splash of extra-virgin olive oil. Add a pinch each kosher salt, red pepper flakes, and cumin seeds, plus one 28-ounce can whole plum tomatoes and bring to a boil; simmer until thick. Stir in greens, then crack in two eggs per person and cover, until the whites are just set.

Canned Coconut Milk

Coconutty Dal

In a saucepan over medium-high heat, sauté 1 chopped shallot, 2 minced garlic cloves, 1 inch minced ginger, and a pinch each ground cumin, coriander, and turmeric in a splash of neutral oil. Add 1 cup dried red lentils, one 13.5-ounce can coconut milk, the can's worth of water, and a pinch of kosher salt. Bring to a boil, then simmer until thick, 15 minutes.

Scallion & Coconut Rice with Pork

In a Dutch oven over medium heat, brown 1 pound ground pork until no longer pink, add a dash of fish sauce. Transfer to a bowl. In the pan, soften 2 sliced scallions and 1 inch minced ginger in a splash of oil, then toast 1¼ cups medium-grain rice until shiny. Add one 13.5-ounce can coconut milk and ½ cup water, bring to a boil; lower heat and cover until rice is tender, 20 minutes. Add the pork.

Pasta e Ceci

In a saucepan over medium heat, fry 2 smashed garlic cloves in a splash of olive oil, then add a couple spoonfuls of tomato paste. Sauté until brick-red, then add one drained 15-ounce can chickpeas, ½ cup small dried pasta (like ditalini), 2 cups boiling water, and a pinch of kosher salt. Simmer, stirring occasionally, until water is absorbed and pasta is tender.

Espinacas con Garbanzos

In a saucepan over medium heat, soften 1 chopped onion and 2 minced garlic cloves in a splash of olive oil. Add 2 tsp cumin seeds, 1 Tbsp tomato paste, and a pinch each smoked paprika, kosher salt, and cayenne, cooking until brick-red. Add one drained 15-ounce can chickpeas, 1 cup stock and simmer for 10 minutes. Stir in one 6-ounce bag baby spinach and let wilt.

Our Test Kitchen's Tricks for Perking Things Up with Pantry Staples

A little personality in the pantry can bring instant vigor to an otherwise straightforward meal. Our test kitchen relies on these flavor-boosting staples day in and day out, and gave us a few ideas for harnessing their spunkiness.

- Crank up chicken soup or meatball mix with a few drops of funky **fish sauce**.

- Stir a spoonful of **chile paste** (like sambal or Calabrian chiles) into olive oil for a spicy all-purpose drizzle (try it on pizza!).

- Dust savory roasted potatoes or stewy chickpeas with lemony, tangy **sumac**.

- Lend earthy, licorice-y sweetness to hearty roasted veggies, chicken, and pork with **fennel seeds**.

For an herbal, floral depth, add a **bay leaf** or two to grains, beans, or potatoes while they cook.

Cook an **anchovy** in hot olive oil with a pinch of chile flakes, then toss with pasta or cooked beans for a quick dinner.

Boost nearly anything you're making (from salad dressings to sauces and braises) by using **pickles** and their pickling liquid. Our test kitchen's partial to pickled onions, beets, or green beans.

Sprinkle a pan of roasted vegetables or scrambled eggs with toasty, savory **nutritional yeast**.

Add a hit of umami to sauces or soups with a tablespoon of **red, yellow, or white miso**.

6 Super-Simple Steps to Stock Your Fridge & Freezer

Keeping the fridge and freezer stocked and ready for anything can feel like a full-time job. But thoughtful shopping makes munching, cooking, and gearing up for meals both easier *and* less wasteful. We have six simple steps for making the refrigerator a welcoming first stop for a snack and the natural destination for cooking inspiration.

1. **Have a running list (with some constants).** Try keeping your most-used items (milk, bananas, kale, eggs) on your grocery list all the time, so it's second nature to pick them up at the store.

2. **Shop in season.** Let what's available guide your menus and your shopping. There's no better way to learn what's in season than browsing a local farmers' market!

3. **Buy the best you can afford—especially when it comes to meat and dairy—and only what you'll use in a week or two.** Better ingredients not only make for a more delicious end result, they also support small producers and animal welfare. Buying only what you'll use lessens food waste.

4. **When you can, shop from specialty counters or retailers.** Pick up cheeses, olives, and charcuterie in the deli department of your grocery store rather than buying prepacked versions. Seek out meat and fish from butchers and fishmongers, if they're available in your community. Turn to farmers' markets or CSAs for produce. You can get (and spend) exactly the amount you want, and it'll be fresher.

5. **Be a prepper.** Prep your produce as soon as you get home from your big shop (see page 54 to learn how). The ingredients will last longer, and you'll have leaped the first hurdle to dinner.

6. **Waste not.** What goes in must go out. Take stock of your fridge and freezer's contents each week and make a note of anything saggy-looking or approaching its best-by date (put them closer to the front of the fridge as an easy reminder). You can throw these things into a frittata, soup, or stir-fry in the days ahead.

Trusty Fridge Companions
for On-the-Fly Meals

The fridge is exactly like your pantry (only cold). Fill it with staples that make it easy to cook a variety of meals on a whim, taking trips to the store just for special or "starring" ingredients (a beautiful salmon fillet; a ripe, juicy heirloom tomato from the farmers' market; or fresh, handmade ravioli from your favorite pasta purveyor). Whether you go with **The Short List** or **The Long List**, we'd start with these items.

The Short List

Produce

- Fresh basil, parsley, and/or cilantro
- Fruit for easy snacking (like berries or apples)
- Lemons and/or limes
- Some kind of hardy green for cooking (like kale or collards)
- Some kind of softer green for salads (like baby spinach or arugula)
- Sturdy aromatics (like carrots or celery)
- Vegetables for roasting (like cauliflower or beets)

Dairy

- Butter
- Cheese for snacking on (like Cheddar or Gouda)
- Milk
- Parmesan and/or pecorino for grating (not pre-grated, please, so it's more versatile)
- Plain whole-milk or Greek yogurt

Meat, Poultry & Other Proteins

- Eggs

Frozen Stuff

- Chicken pieces (whatever parts you most like to eat)
- Fresh sausages for cooking (whole or loose)
- Frozen berries or other fruit (like mango or pineapple)
- Frozen peas or other versatile, multipurpose vegetables (like spinach or edamame)
- Ground beef
- Sliced bacon

CONTINUED

The Long List

Produce

- Avocados (kept on the counter until ripe)
- Ginger (fresh)
- In-season produce that will take center stage in your cooking
- Olives (fresh from the olive bar or jarred)
- Rosemary or thyme (fresh)
- Scallions

Dairy

- Accent cheese (like ricotta, feta, or Gorgonzola)
- Nondairy milk

Meat, Poultry & Other Proteins

- Charcuterie (like cured sausages or sliced salami)
- Firm tofu

Frozen Stuff

- Fish fillets (like salmon or cod, and/or shrimp)
- Homemade chicken or vegetable stock
- Instant dry yeast (it lasts forever in the freezer!)
- Jalapeños or other chiles (they freeze gorgeously and thaw almost instantly)

Other

- Chile paste (like sambal, gochujang, or harissa)
- Corn or flour tortillas
- Fish sauce
- Kimchi, sauerkraut, and/or pickles
- Miso paste (red, yellow, or white, ranging from funkiest to mildest)
- Preserved lemons

SOME THINGS DON'T BELONG IN THE FRIDGE!

This includes tomatoes (they actually get *worse* in there), potatoes, bananas, unripe avocados, stone fruits (except for cherries), onions and shallots, garlic, whole pineapples, melons, and basil. Keep them on the counter instead and use before they get soft or squishy.

To Freeze or Not to Freeze?

Yes, your freezer will hold you over for the long haul, but it wants to be a regular weeknight hero, too! Below you'll find some yes-ways and no-gos to guide you as your fill 'er up. Just take care to label and date everything that goes in (and visit page 54 for our tips on storage, including preventing freezer burn).

Safe to Freeze & Thaw

Fruits, vegetables & other staples

- Blanched, boiled, or roasted vegetables
- Butter
- Egg whites and yolks (frozen in their own freezer-safe containers, or in ice-cube trays as described on page 54)
- Hard cheeses
- Milk
- Most fruits (peeled and chopped)
- Scraps for making stock (like carrot tops and chicken bones)
- Uncooked meat or fish that hasn't been previously frozen

Savories

- Baked pastas and casseroles
- Braised meats or meatballs in sauce
- Cooked beans in their liquid
- Cooked breaded chicken cutlets
- Cooked or oil-based sauces (like marinara, pesto, and curry paste)
- Soups, stews, and chilis

Sweets & baked stuff

- Baked muffins, scones, breads, and cakes
- Portioned cookies at any stage, baked or unbaked
- Unbaked yeasted doughs

Never Freeze & Thaw

- Apples, citrus fruits, or melon
- Chocolate
- Coffee in an opened bag or canister
- Most fried foods
- Raw produce with a high water content (like romaine, cucumbers, and celery)
- Raw whole eggs in their shells
- Soft or semisoft cheeses
- Uncooked potatoes
- Yogurt

WHEN FREEZING IN GLASS . . .
Take care to leave lots of space for the liquid to expand—at least ½ inch from the container's lip. Glass pushed to its limit will shatter, and, geez Louise, what a mess that is to clean up. When it's time to thaw, let the contents unfreeze at least partially (on their own in the refrigerator, or at room temperature before microwaving or thawing in a water bath) so as not to shock the glass.

Life Preservers: How to Keep Things Fresh in the Fridge & Freezer

Stocking a fridge and freezer requires a little bit of strategy: What deserves a piece of that valuable real estate? And just how long can the freezer work its fountain-of-youth magic? Give your fresh and frozen goods a long, happy life with these tips.

In the Fridge

- **Anything with a leafy top (like carrots, beets, and fennel)** should have the greens removed before storing. (You can eat the greens, too—wash, dry, and store as below.)

- **Apples and pears** (plus cantaloupes, ripe bananas, peaches, plums, tomatoes, potatoes, and more) emit a gas (ethylene!) that can speed up the ripening of other produce. Store them separately, and everything will last longer.

- **Berries** should take a bath in a mild vinegar solution (3 parts water to 1 part white vinegar) before being stored in the fridge in a kitchen towel–lined bowl. Vinegar's acidity kills any spores potentially growing on the fruit, keeping them bacteria-free and fresh.

- **Cheeses** should be wrapped tightly in porous, breathable parchment paper or cheese wrap (or put into a special cheese vault!) between uses. Plastic wrap or ziplock bags will suffocate the cheese and encourage bacterial growth.

- **Greens** should be washed, dried, stemmed, and stored in a breathable bag or storage bin.

- **Herbs** should also be washed and dried, wrapped in a damp kitchen towel, and tucked into a breathable bag or bin.

- **Leftovers** are best stored in see-through, airtight containers (page 25 has our recs).

- **Nut oils** (and whole nuts) will have twice the lifespan in the fridge than in the pantry. You can store them in their original packaging, but make sure to seal them well—and date them, please! (See pages 42 to 43 for their lifespan.)

In the Freezer

- **Freeze small amounts of leftover liquids, sauces, and aromatics in an ice-cube tray** (once initially frozen, remove them from the molds and store them in a freezer-safe container or bag). Think tomato paste for sauce, leftover wine for risotto, or mashed roasted garlic for creamy pasta.

- **Make sure everything freezer-bound is totally, completely cool before freezing.** Hot foods will bring up the temp of the whole freezer, which is not the safest for that salmon you're saving.

- **Protect against freezer burn by tightly wrapping cooked food** (like baked goods or non-saucy stuff) in plastic or beeswax wrap, then in aluminum foil.

A Look Inside the Fridges of 4 Food52ers

Opening the pantry of a cook whose food we love to eat makes us want to snoop around in their fridge, too, and then hightail it to the grocery store to stock up on new favorite ingredients. Four cooks we adore shared all—and a couple of their go-to meals—with us. Peek at what was inside.

EMMA LAPERRUQUE, FOOD WRITER & BIG LITTLE RECIPE DEVELOPER

- **Cooked brown rice—and a lot of it.** I eat it with breakfast, lunch, and dinner.

- **Prewashed and cut kale.** Is this cheating? I don't care! It keeps for days, rounds out so many meals, and saves me time when I get home from work and need food *now*.

- **White or rosé wine, beer, and, most important, dirty martini ingredients.**

- **Tofu or tempeh**, probably both.

- **Miso**, both white and red.

- **So much butter**—unsalted for baking and cultured-salted for spreading.

- **Cheese!** Something grilled cheese–friendly, like Cheddar; something hard and grate-able, like Parm or pecorino; and crumbly, sharp feta.

- **Pickles.** Bread-and-butter for my husband, Justin, and cornichons for me.

- **Oil-cured olives.** For pastas and salads, aka most of what I eat.

- **So. Many. Condiments.** But I need them (don't I?). Many, many spicy things: Sriracha, Cholula, Lao Gan Ma chili crisp, crushed Calabrian chiles in oil, chile bean paste, and prepared horseradish. Plus: Soy sauce. Worcestershire. Sesame oil. Ketchup. Dijon mustard. Nut/seed butters (peanut, almond, tahini). Jam. Mayo. Better than Bouillon (chicken and vegetable).

Back-Pocket Dinners from Emma's Fridge

→ Brown rice bowl with sautéed kale, scrambled eggs, crumbled roasted seaweed, and spicy mayo.

→ Whole-wheat pasta with salted butter, ground pecorino, lots of black pepper, and a roasted vegetable (probably broccoli).

→ Tacos with crispy tempeh nuggets, along with Greek yogurt, shredded lettuce, and hot sauce. Maybe a side salad, too.

ERIC KIM, FOOD EDITOR (& MASTER AT COOKING FOR ONE)

- I always have some **leftover cooked rice.** As soon as I make rice in the cooker, I transfer it to a container so it doesn't yellow or get too crunchy in the pot (a habit I picked up from my mother). The "warm" setting is the demise of good rice!

- **Tuscan kale** in the crisper drawer because it stays fresh for much longer than curly kale. I also prefer its hearty texture.

- **Seltzer and white wine**, for spritzes.

- **Cut-up carrots**, for a quick snack (and because my dog likes them, too).

- A tub of **cottage cheese**, because I think it's great to munch on (contrary to popular opinion!). I also like to use it in pancakes.

CONTINUED

- **Kimchi,** which I buy in huge containers and eat on rice, in soups, and with noodles. If I make it at home, it's always my mom's recipe and in big quantities since the process is so labor-intensive no matter what the yield.

- **My Instant Pot insert,** full of leftovers and topped with foil. Usually I'll make a big portion of soup, stew, or curry so I don't have to cook every day.

- **Eggs.** I eat a single 6-minute egg every morning for breakfast (and go through a dozen a week!).

- **Maple syrup,** great in salad dressings and on candied bacon alike.

Back-Pocket Dinners from Eric's Fridge

→ **Kimchi fried rice,** using the huge container of kimchi and leftover white rice in my fridge. There's usually a can of Spam in my pantry to go in it, too; and a final sprinkle of furikake and a fried egg usually go on top.

→ **Cottage cheese pancakes,** because sometimes I just want a classic breakfast. The ones I make are packed with protein (eggs, cottage cheese, plus a little flour, salt, and baking powder), and taste like little cheesecakes. Since the recipe is so forgiving, it's easy to scale down—often, I'll just make enough batter for two pancakes.

→ For late nights, it's often a package of **instant ramen.** I boil the ramen noodles (saving the seasoning pack for later), drain them, and stir in some Lao Gan Ma chili crisp, which dyes the noodles a glorious burnt umber and scents the dish with spicy, garlicky goodness. I'm obsessed. A single poached egg is also involved, of course.

ALLISON BRUNS BUFORD, TALENTED TEST KITCHEN DIRECTOR

- **Whole milk and whole-milk Greek yogurt.** I personally prefer them to the low-fat varieties, and as they're most often called for in recipes, you've already got them on hand!

- **Flavored kefir.** Great for easy overnight oats.

- **Beer.** Treat yourself! I'm also not above keeping a boxed rosé in the fridge during the summer.

- **Eggs.** If you have these in the house, a meal is never far away.

- **Unsalted butter for baking, and salted Irish butter for toast.** The block in the fridge is just a refill for the French butter keeper we leave on the counter.

- **Scallions.** I don't usually have fresh herbs hanging around unless I'm making a specific recipe, but I do make an exception for scallions. They add color and an herbaceous zip to any dish.

- **Fresh pasta.** It's better in flavor and texture than dried, and it cooks in minutes.

- **Cooked veggies and prewashed fruit.** Now you're good to go!

Back-Pocket Dinners from Allison's Fridge

→ **Baked salmon with rice and Cheat's Vietnamese Caramel Sauce** (recipe found on Food52.com). The sauce is really the star here, made with fridge and pantry staples: soy sauce, fish sauce, brown sugar, and mashed ginger (in a tube!). Put some sauce and the fish in a baking dish while the oven heats to 350°F, then stick the whole thing in the oven for about 15 minutes. Spoon any extra sauce over salmon and cooked rice, plus whatever cooked veg you might have.

→ **Fried rice.** A simple and satisfying solution for leftovers, like rice from a previous meal and that quarter of a pork tenderloin left in the fridge. Frozen peas are always around to add some green if desired. This is also where those scallions in my crisper drawer come in handy.

→ **Shakshuka.** With quality canned tomatoes and some eggs, the possibilities are nearly limitless. Maybe I'll dress it up for dinner with some harissa, grains, and/or greens. And remember that whole-milk Greek yogurt I always keep? It becomes a shortcut labneh!

EMILY CONNOR (AKA EMILYC), SALAD ALL-STAR

- **Lemons and limes.** You'll always find these. I use citrus in practically everything I cook.

- **Italian parsley.** It's such an easy way to add freshness and brightness to anything.

- **Butter.** A necessity for cooking and baking alike. I recently switched to salted (for everything!) and will never go back.

- **Eggs.** A must for baking and busy weeknights.

- **Whole-milk yogurt.** I turn to it for so many things: quick breakfasts, smoothies, marinades, salad dressings, and more.

- **Various types of cheese**—sharp Cheddar, mozzarella, and Parmesan are musts.

- **Mayo**—always full-fat Duke's!

- **Pickled, briny things.** I love these, so you'll always find olives, capers, dill pickles, and preserved lemons in my fridge.

Back-Pocket Dinners from Emily's Fridge

→ **Fried egg sandwiches,** which are a go-to for us on harried weeknights. I like to fry them in olive oil so they get super-crispy edges, then play around with the toppings: different cheeses, spicy stuff (like harissa), or greens piled on top.

→ **Quesadillas,** which are so simple and customizable—not to mention one of the best ways to use up bits and bobs from the fridge. My kids love theirs with leftover meat and cheese, while mine get packed full of roasted or sautéed vegetables, like broccoli or Brussels sprouts. We always make them with soft flour tortillas and serve them with salted yogurt on the side.

→ **Sheet-pan salads,** where vegetables are roasted together on a rimmed sheet pan and tossed with a simple dressing and fresh accents at the end. While I'm constantly changing up the vegetables (like butternut squash in the fall and asparagus in the spring), I frequently add cheese, nuts, and something briny (like olives or capers), and toss in fresh herbs (like parsley) before serving.

The Big Stock-Up: Our Tips for Shopping, Sourcing & Investing

Decisions about how to budget for groceries can be exhausting and intimidating, but that's where your smart-shopper skills come in. Determine what's most important to you—maybe it's buying humanely raised meat, packing homemade lunches for your kids, supporting local farmers as much as you possibly can, or eating simply through the week and throwing a rockin' dinner party on Saturday night. Prioritize and then plan your grocery list around what budget's left.

What to Buy in Bulk

For the staples you lean on day in and day out, you want a balance: high quality (you're eating them all the time, after all!) at a lower price (because, ahem, you're eating them *all* the time). Whether online or at wholesale clubs, specialty counters, or dedicated big-box stores, you can get a good deal on great stuff by buying a lot at once—win, win!

- Flats or multipacks of dried pasta
- Flats of canned or boxed staples, (tomatoes, beans, lentils, and such)
- Grains (like rice, oats, quinoa, and farro)
- Nuts and dried fruit

What to Buy Generic

At your neighborhood grocery store, you can easily pick up the one-off ingredients you need a relatively small amount of at any given time. These ingredients are roughly the same quality regardless of the producer, so feel free to buy the generic version (or whichever brand you like best).

- Butter (for cooking and baking)
- Briny things (like pickles and capers)
- Canned and bottled once-in-a-whiles (like coconut milk)
- Flour
- Neutral oil
- Sugar

What to Invest In

These are the ingredients we think it's worth budgeting extra for, and that's because the quality of the food (and, in the case of animal products, the quality of animal welfare) is substantially better. Buying from specialty markets vendors gets you closer to the supply chain.

Animal products
- Butter (for spreading)
- Canned or jarred tuna, anchovies, and sardines
- Charcuterie
- Cheeses
- Eggs
- Fresh meat and seafood
- Milk
- Yogurt

Fruit & veg
- Jam
- Produce of all sorts

Pantry staples
- Chocolate
- Coffee and tea
- Olive oil
- Spices

ORGANIC, SUSTAINABLE? FREE-RANGE, LOCAL? WHAT'S BEST?!

This topic is . . . complicated, to say the least. It's not always doable to eat locally, and we can't always shop at the farmers' market. But whenever we can, we prioritize humanely raised animal products, organic produce, and fair-trade or local makers. Aside from reading the labels, just ask the producer about your food. You can learn about its origin, the environment it's made in (like how the farm raises its animals and produce, or what the factory's sustainability practices are), and much more.

We've got a few more suggestions for how to shop thoughtfully, and on any kind of budget:

- **Check the labels.** At the grocery store, you'll find seals that indicate an item was grown, harvested, or made responsibly and ethically. Some labels to look for are Rainforest Alliance Certified, Leaping Bunny, PETA'S Cruelty-Free, MSC Certified sustainable seafood.

- **Join a food co-op.** Depending on the co-op, you may have to invest a few hours of work each month—but you'll be rewarded with deep discounts.

- **Go in on bulk online orders with friends.** This is an especially good option for those who live a ways from grocery stores. Get the benefit of wholesale pricing by placing large orders together from national retailers (like Frontier, Mountain Rose Herbs, Unfi, and Thrive Market), then splitting the goods (and the cost).

- **Explore what your farmers' market offers.** Many vendors sell discounted produce that's a little bent out of shape (called "seconds," and it's perfectly delicious to eat!). Some vendors even accept EBT/food stamps/SNAP benefits. Sharing a CSA with friends is another way to make the most of the farmers' market without spending a lot.

Cookbook Author
NIK SHARMA'S
Inspired Kitchen (& Pantry)

Nik Sharma is the author and photographer of James Beard Award-nominated cookbook *Season*. We love his soulful recipes, which are influenced by his North Indian and Goan heritage, and his Californian home. Nik gave us a tour of his light, bright kitchen that overlooks the garden he tends himself. In the kitchen, he uses his ample counter space to store larger tools and ingredients he works with frequently, and to display his beautiful cookware. For the rest—including his extensive spice collection and precious cookbook library—Nik organizes what he can in cabinets and then gets creative with wall-mounted shelving outside of the immediate cooking space.

→ **In my pantry**, I keep many different grains and lentils, coconut milk and cream, sweetened condensed milk, and beans. I also keep a separate shelf for sweeteners (jaggery, maple syrup, honey, golden syrup), cocoa powders and chocolate, dried fruit, and tamarind pulp.

→ **As for fridge staples:** milk, yogurt, kefir and buttermilk, eggs. Brined pickles as well as Indian *achar* (pickles preserved in oil and spices), and large batches of homemade ghee. **In the freezer:** frozen berries and an assortment of nut flours.

One thing I strongly recommend is to **decant** most things and **label everything** with its name and purchase date. Try to **organize by kind** or at least **keep similar things all together**. To this end, I label all my spices, even the ones that I regularly use.

In the fridge, I like to **sort and store by ingredient type**; it makes it easier to shop and cook because I can easily get an idea of what's running low.

I love to garden, and mostly grow herbs, fruit, and vegetables I like to eat—but there is the odd herb that I want to cook with for fun. (My latest addition is a makrut lime tree.)

USE THIS
CHAPTER

To Find a
Home for
Every Kitchen
Helper

CHAPTER 3

Storing
& Organizing

A kitchen's organizational system doesn't need to be perfect;
it just has to support the cooks who use it. You don't have to
buy a bunch of matching bins if that's not your style. There are
lots of ways to organize—baskets, shelves, racks, bins, jars,
and beyond!—and the quirks are what make a kitchen uniquely
geared for you. In this chapter, we cover all things decluttering,
storing, and organizing tools and ingredients, plus how to come
up with systems that work for you and your space.

Meet the Rhombus

Take a look around your kitchen. What shape is it? What are the parts of it you visit most? They're probably the **sink**, the **fridge**, and the **stove**—a trio so ubiquitous that designers and architects call it "the triangle." We'd add the **counter** as a fourth destination, making our kitchen a . . . rhombus. This well-worn rhomboid groove consists of the most productive spots in the space. Internalize these four zones, and what happens at each—we'll tell you how to make the most of them on page 66.

Counter: Chopping, peeling, organizing, jotting lists, fixing up a meal (your primary workspace)

Stove/Oven: Boiling water, roasting a chicken, simmering soups all afternoon

Sink: Doing the dishes, filling glasses, arranging flowers, washing greens

Fridge: Stocking groceries, stashing leftovers, figuring out what to cook

5 Tips for Sharpening Up Your Route Through the Kitchen

There's lots that can be done to make your path more easily traveled, or to make each "stop" more productive. The less running back and forth you have to do, the more seamless your cooking will be. You probably already do some of these things intuitively.

1. **Embrace the rhombus.** Give each station equal importance by making it as efficient (and pleasant to be at) as possible. That might mean adding a cushioned mat in front of the counter to make Sunday meal prep more comfortable. Or, try storing mixing bowls, storage containers, and a compost bin on or near the counter. The sink might be stocked with soaps, brushes, kitchen towels, *and* hand lotion. Pans, cooking utensils, and ingredients want to be near the stove, along with your recipe cards and cookbooks.

2. **Then go beyond it.** What else do you use your kitchen for? Homework? Eating? Cocktail parties? Consider making "stations" for those uses: a desk complete with a jar full of pens and a bin for wrangling charging cords; a cozy spot to sit for a meal, with a stash of napkins and placemats; a dedicated drawer of corkscrews, toothpicks, and tea lights.

3. **Think about what you use most often—and what you don't.** If you can, keep only what you use daily out on the counter. Organize cabinets and shelves so that your most-reached-for tools and ingredients are up front. (After you've whirled through the kitchen like the organizing wizard you are, we bet you'll find more than a few things you don't need anymore. Head to page 28 for a how-to on decluttering, and to page 87 to find out how to donate them.)

4. **Get creative in smaller spaces.** A freestanding cart (topped with a butcher block or otherwise) can transform a countertopless kitchen, creating a prep zone you don't have to move anything to access (with extra storage on the shelves below).

5. **Make inefficient corners earn their keep.** A storage solution can turn an awkward space into an essential one. If you've got countertop area to spare, make part of it into a bar or breakfast corner or letter-writing station. Hidden or slim nooks can stash your mop and broom, and too-high or too-low shelves can show off favorite cookbooks, a row of beloved trinkets, or pretty cookware.

Carving Out Your Workspace (the Kitchen's Busiest Spot!)

A tidy, organized workspace eliminates any and all obstacles to cooking. With everything you need just an arm's length away, you can simply jump into whatever delicious task you fancy. These guidelines will lead you to a streamlined workspace—one where you can whisk up a vinaigrette, stem and tear greens, and season a piece of meat, all with elbow room to spare.

What *Should* Be in Your Kitchen Workspace

- A rack or block of knives

- A crock or mounted rail with larger essentials, like wooden spoons and silicone spatulas

- A drawer of smaller essentials, like measuring cups and vegetable peelers

- A butcher block you can chop directly on, or a nearby stack of cutting boards

- A drawer, cabinet, rack, or pegboard of mixing bowls and most used pots and pans

- A small tray or lazy Susan of basics to get your cooking going, like salt and pepper, oil, vinegar, and favorite spices

What *Shouldn't* Be in Your Kitchen Workspace

- Papers, including mail, dry-cleaning receipts, work or personal documents, the newspaper, and your kid's field-trip permission slip

- Your computer and its charger

- Purses, bags, or backpacks

- Kitchen tools and appliances that aren't used daily (like stand mixers or juicers)

ODE TO THE JUNK DRAWER

We *love* a junk drawer—it helps our main workspace stay organized and clutter-free. So what should go in there? All the little doodads you need on hand that don't have much to do with cooking (think notepads, rubber bands, batteries, that jumble of clips you fasten chip bags with). House them in **shallow boxes**, on **trays**, or in **drawer dividers** to keep the chaos controlled.

6 Workspace Strategies That Keep Our Test Kitchen Humming

The test kitchen is the heart of the Food52 office. On a busy day, it can see up to twenty wildly different recipes, divided among as many as four cooks. That's a heavy load for a little kitchen to bear, and it's possible thanks to a few key features. We've identified the six things we love best about this space—including a few you can lift for your own home.

2. **Multiple workspaces**—two long sets of countertops on either side of a single aisle—allow multiple chefs to move and work freely without too much bumping of elbows. If you cook with your whole family, an extra workspace (hi again, kitchen cart) can give everyone breathing room.

3. **Good lighting** makes the space pleasant to be in. In your kitchen, use bright white lightbulbs (rather than warm white) for a cheerful atmosphere; the better to see your knife work, too.

1. **Low, open storage racks** beneath some of the countertops keep heavy, oft-used pots and pans within reach, show them off, and keep air circulating around them so they dry more quickly. Get this at home with a freestanding kitchen cart or worktable with a roomy countertop and shelving beneath.

5. **A rolling speed rack** (a tall metal rack that can hold many sheet pans at once) is a restaurant essential that's also at home in the test kitchen. The cooks load it with multiple projects in various stages, eliminating the need for cooling racks and also keeping the counters clear.

6. **In-drawer knife blocks** lay flat in the drawers alongside other tools, giving the test kitchen's expansive knife collection a safe place to hang out when not in use. Our kitchen likes the ones from Messermeister.

4. **Smart, thoughtfully designed cabinetry** fits larger tools, bowls, and some appliances (like the blender and food processor), thanks to adjustable shelves. The doors have a cushioned close, which makes for a lot less slamming. You may not be able to hack adjustable shelves without some home renovation, but you can easily get quieter cabinets: Add a couple of stick-on, sound-dampening door bumpers, which you can find at the hardware store.

How to Organize Your Everyday Stuff
(Or, How to Unjumble the Jumble)

Now that you've set yourself up with everything you need, it's time to keep it from ending up in a big pile. So ask yourself: What do you use most often, and where do you use it? Does it have a "family" of similar items? How easy is it to access? With this in mind, here are our go-to organizing tools and strategies.

- **Trays** wrangle and anchor "sets"—like your daily tea-making supplies near the kettle or your salt, pepper, and oil near the stove.

- **Mini organizing baskets** and **drawer dividers** turn jumbled drawers into orderly ones. These are great for utensils and the small, handheld stuff (your can opener, church key, thermometer, and such).

- **Narrow wall-mounted spice racks, plate hangers, hanging plate racks,** or even **picture rails** show off dishware in style (they're like art you can eat on!), especially when grouped together by color.

- **Dish risers** create storage space out of thin air.

- **Hanging or freestanding shelves** display the prettiest (and biggest) of your tool kit—like pitchers, teapots, and cake stands.

- **Vertical plate holders** secure wobbly stacks of dishes in drawers or on shelves.

- **Cup hooks** work for mugs, sure, but also for oft-grabbed tools.

- **Hooks** give a home to kitchen towels, apron straps, baskets, and shopping totes.

- **Mounted Shaker-style peg rails** or **curtain wire hung like a laundry line** will hold anything that can be dangled from an S-hook—like towels, scissors, cup measures, or a braid of garlic.

Out-of-Our-Way Methods
for Storing Pots & Pans

Where to put the pots and pans we reach for daily, for maximum convenience and minimal hefting? We've got a bunch of ideas:

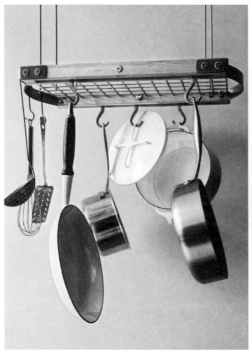

- Dangling from a **hanging pot rack** suspended from the ceiling

- Lined up along a **metal kitchen rail with S-hooks**

- . . . Or along a **Shaker-style wooden rail**

- Hung on a **pegboard**

- Stacked on or parading along the **shelves of a bookshelf or cart**

Plus, here are five ways to tidy their lids:

- Tucked behind a **mounted metal rail**

- Lined up in an **accordion rack**

- Stored upside down **in their corresponding pots**

- Stashed on a **cabinet door–mounted lid rack**

- Stood upright in the slatted shelves of a **wire shelving unit**

How to Make Bulky Tools & Appliances Disappear (Well, Sort of . . .)

Much as we like a minimalist space and airy, wide-open countertops, it often makes sense to leave the larger helpers be (think the toaster and electric kettle you use every day, or the hard-to-move microwave). You can make them part of a tableau: Surround them with things you *do* like to look at, like plants, art, and your cookbook collection. Or situate them among other oft-used tools—beneath a pegboard, for instance—so they look like part of a coordinated crew.

For the rest, the things that need a home *off* the counter? Arrange them alone or in groups . . .

- In your **deepest drawers**, or on **tall or slide-out cabinet shelves** (Bonus: If you have the option to fit your cabinets with electrical outlets, run with it! Fill them with appliances you'll never have to remove to use.)

- On **bookshelves** or the **low-level shelves of your island**

- On the **shelves of your pantry** (as long as they don't push out other ingredients by being there)

- On a **utility cart** that you can tuck away in a big closet—or embrace as part of your kitchen décor

- In a **built-in cabinet** or **freestanding armoire** all their own

- On **extra-high shelves, on top of the fridge** or in the **gap between the cabinets and ceiling**

4 Strategies for Conquering Storage-Container Mountain

We're guessing you're plenty familiar with the woes of wrestling food-storage containers—round pegs in square holes, mismatched lids and bowls, plus the odd leftover takeout box. With four simple steps, you can make sense of your situation, once and for all.

1. **Pull all of your storage containers out** of wherever they live, and match tops with bottoms. Toss or donate any strays, recycle plastic takeout containers, which usually aren't microwave- or dishwasher-safe, and be ruthless with anything stained, smelly, or misshapen.

2. **Review what you've got left** (and what you need), considering your cooking and eating habits. Glance at our starter kit on page 25 for guidelines on stocking up.

3. Once you've established who stays, who leaves, and who else is invited, **stack like and like together**: round with round, square with square, neatly nesting them.

4. **Devote a low, wide drawer or a cabinet or pantry shelf to your containers**, so you can see what you've got and protect against avalanches. If you're working with deep shelves, keep containers you use most up front and lesser-used ones behind.

Those Rascally Lids!

Now that the bottoms have a home, you'll want a few places to keep the lids, ahem, contained:

- A **deep-sided tray, small basket or bin**, or **fabric box** that can nestle up against the stacked containers.

- A **basket** or a **magazine holder hooked over a cabinet door**, or installed on its inside.

- A **clip-on storage basket or shelf** (yep, we'll use up every inch of that prime vertical space below), and/or a **plate rack** where lids can "stack" horizontally.

Organizing the Pantry (Or, How to Keep the Madness Contained)

We know the pantry's a tool kit: an intentional, supremely functional set of ingredients (and some snacks, too). But pantries can be plagued by tippy boxes and bags, shadowy corners, dusty messes—or worse yet, pests (yikes!). To ward off pantry chaos, we ask our three essential questions: What do you use most often? Does it have a "family" of similar items it can go with? How easy it is to access? We like a mix of lots of different organizational tools that give us a flexible system to maneuver through it all (plus, see page 78 for tips on storing individual ingredients).

- **High-sided trays** are great for anything that a taller edge would help keep contained—like all your boxed and canned tomato purées and sauces, or your stand mixer and all of its attachments.

- **Large airtight, lidded glass or plastic canisters** (from 1 liter to 5 liters or larger) to house bulk ingredients, like flour, and snacks, like granola bars; stackable is best for these, too.

- **Lazy Susans** make hard-to-reach cabinet corners valuable real estate.

- **Lidded glass jam, mason, and paint jars** in a variety of sizes (from tiny 1-ounce jars to liter size or larger—and stackable, please!) store spices, nuts, grains, beans, and more.

- **Over-door racks** transform nothing space into storage for spices and canned goods.

- **Small cardboard or shoe boxes** do just the same!

- **Wire or woven baskets** collect puffy bags of chips, stacks of kitchen towels, or a family of various bottles.

Whip Your Pantry into Shape with These 7 Steps

Most of us hear the call to organize our pantries and try as hard as we possibly can to tune that call out. No more! These seven steps will get you a pantry setup to be proud of.

1. **Pull everything out.** Yep, *everything*, from all the shelves, and dust them all off (shelves, too). Toss or compost ingredients you haven't cooked with in a while (and don't plan on returning to), food gifts you received but won't use, and anything past its best-by date.

2. **Decant ingredients and check inventory.** You know by now how much we love airtight containers, especially those you can see into (and *especially* if they stack!). As you decant, make a list of ingredients that need a top-off.

3. **Protect against invaders.** We're talking pests of all kinds. Embrace airtight containers. Freeze pantry items as soon as you purchase them to kill any existing critters or their eggs. Tackle crumbs and sticky spots as they happen (see page 138 for how).

4. **Clearly label your stores.** With ingredients that have a short shelf life, you may find it helpful to include the date you purchased it. Pull out your trusty label maker or fall back on Old Faithful, aka painter's tape and a permanent marker.

5. **Group items in "families."** Think canned things, pasta and grains, and nuts and dried fruit. Arrange them on the same shelf or group them in a basket or bin. A "baking specifics" bin might include baking powder and soda, vanilla extract, cocoa powder, chocolate chips, and muffin-tin liners.

6. **Position most-used staples within easy sight and reach.** If you can't see it, chances are you won't use it. (Stash what you use least on higher-up shelves— a stepstool's your friend!)

7. **Rinse and repeat as necessary.** At least every six months or so. If you're just not using an item, give it to a friend or donate it to a food pantry. (Just check the expiration date.)

THE EVERY-NOW- & THEN-ERS

We see you, pasta roller and pastry bags. Corral tools you use less regularly in a small lidded storage bin and label what's inside (e.g., "Christmas cookie cutters"). Put the box on a high-up shelf for when you'll use it next.

And for those large, unwieldy items that you pull out only for your biggest parties and gatherings (hi, roasting pans and chafing dishes)? Tuck them into large bins (labeled with the contents, please) and hide them out of sight, even outside the kitchen. Or embrace nice-looking storage solutions you can keep out, like benches with hidden cavities, vintage steamer trunks, or attractive fabric or wood bins.

Going Rogue: How to Make a Pantry in Any Kind of Kitchen

A spacious, walk-in pantry for all of our staples is the stuff of dreams, for most. But smaller spaces can be just as effective. Here are some clever ways to house cans, jars, and such.

- **Cabinet drawers, both deep and shallow:** Oft-neglected in pantry planning, but great for anything you'd like a bird's-eye view of—jarred spices, dry goods, even cans. Label lids so you can see them from above.

- **Industrial-style metal utility carts:** A nice option for overflow, or a specialized variety of goods (your extensive collection of baking supplies, perhaps). Even better if it's wheeled, so it can become a traveling or disappearing pantry.

- **Freestanding cupboards:** Shelves and pullout drawers you can shut the doors on.

- **Old-school, library-style shelf dividers:** These can help keep different groups contained.

- **Open shelving:** If you can't beat it (a lack of built-in storage, that is), highlight it. Hung shelves, a sturdy bookshelf, or a wire restaurant-style rack make for attractive pantry stand-ins. (Have formal storage but want to open things up? Take your kitchen cabinets' doors off their hinges.)

The Lean, Mean Pantry Behind Our Test Kitchen

The Food52 test kitchen's pantry is inspired by the one in our cofounder Amanda Hesser's Brooklyn home (see page 88 for more about it!). Chef-in-residence (and former test kitchen director) Josh Cohen knows it well.

- **"We have large bulk storage for sugar and various flours and then we organize the rest of the pantry by shelf,"** says Josh. There's one shelf for nuts and dried fruit, one for pastry items (cocoa powder, food coloring, beans for blind baking), a slide-out shelf for vinegars and honey and other condiments, another slide-out shelf for dry spices, a shelf for specialty flours, and a shelf for baking tools (like loaf, springform, and tart pans).

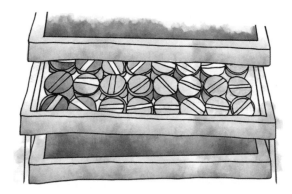

- **All ingredients are transferred from their original packaging as soon as they come in.** Most find a new home in a plastic quart or pint container. Josh says, "For larger bulk storage, I like to use rectangular Cambro containers" (large, heavy-duty storage staples of restaurant kitchens). At home, he uses glass mason jars.

- **Spices are poured into 4-ounce tins with clear tops.** Since they live together on a shallow slide-out shelf (that's a solution lifted straight from Amanda's kitchen), it's easy to see at a glance what's what. And, of course, they get a label, too.

- **Shelves that can be repositioned at different heights are a *must*.** This lets our kitchen team adjust the shelves as necessary to fit growing stacks of pans or an extra-tall bottle of vinegar.

- **Last, mental mise en place is the name of the game.** Above all, the test kitchen stores the items they use the most in places that are easiest to reach. Then they consistently phase out the stuff *not* being used (weekly, in fact!) "We want the kitchen to be as lean and functional as possible," Josh says. "When our shelves have clarity and room, our minds are calm, we're happier, and our cooking improves."

A FEW MORE WAYS TO STORE SPICES . . .

No matter which way you go, labeling is a must—and you can try alphabetizing, color-coding with washi tape, or grouping them by family, too.

- **An over-door wire rack of shelves** is great for those with really big spice collections

- **A deep-sided tray** that can be slid onto a shelf

- **A shallow drawer**

- **A pretty tray on the counter** for most-used spices (or try a masala dabba, a compartmentalized Indian spice tray with a lid)

- **Magnetized containers** that stick to the fridge or to a mounted steel plate

Order! Order! Creating Calm in the Fridge & Freezer

An orderly fridge and freezer work *for* you, not the other way around. It's more *I know what we're having for dinner!* and less *What the heck is this slimy thing?* Here are some of our foolproof ways to stay organized.

First things first:

1. Remove everything from both the fridge and freezer so you can better assess what you have. Toss anything that's past its prime or spiky with ice, that you can't remember buying or using, and that doesn't make you excited to cook or eat.

2. Give the shelves (and any jars or bottles that need it) a quick wipe down with a hot soapy cloth. Head to page 125 if the fridge or freezer needs a more thorough cleaning.

3. Time to put everything back! Here's how.

In the Fridge

Line the bottoms of any crisper drawers with clean kitchen towels to help absorb excess moisture. (No drawers? DIY with lidded, shoebox-size, clear-plastic tubs.)

Then store as follows:

- **Organize like with like.** Peanut butter goes with the jam, hot sauces with their brethren, leftovers stacked all in one place, lunchmeat alongside the cheeses.

  → **Embrace FIFO.** That's *first in, first out,* or the practice of rotating food as it comes in. It might feel less convenient to start, but by putting the newest food at the back and the oldest up front, you'll reach for the ingredients to use up first.

- **Think about the fridge's "zones."**

  → **The crisper drawers** are the coldest and most humid parts of the fridge, and the ideal space for lush vegetables: broccoli and cauliflower, leafy greens, radishes, celery, green beans, and ears of corn in their silky jackets.

  → **The top shelf and the door** are the warmest areas of the fridge and should be home to hardier things—like most condiments and produce that prefers less moisture (think cucumbers, peppers, zucchini, and eggplant).

- **And as for where to put specific ingredients?**

  → **Fruit** should have its own home, whether in a crisper drawer or in a bowl, where it's easily reached for snacking.

  → **Leftovers** and soon-to-expire things should be labeled clearly and dated in airtight containers or mason jars. Store at eye level so you'll use them up.

  → **Lemons and limes** can live in the crisper drawer, too—or in a small bowl that you can pull easily from the fridge while you cook.

CONTINUED

→ **Meat** should be on the bottom shelf. It's the coldest place in the fridge, and putting meat here prevents it from dripping onto anything else.

→ **Milk and other perishables** should live off the door (which is one of the fridge's warmest spots).

In the Freezer

• **Store stuff by family.** This means coordinating ingredients (frozen cubes of homemade stock, tomato paste, or caramelized onions), sauces (pomodoro and pesto), baked goods, meats, vegetables, and so forth.

• **Label before you freeze**, rather than removing something already frozen, then labeling and replacing it in the freezer. The condensation on already-frozen items makes adhesive labels (or painter's tape) pretty much ineffective, but as long as the label goes on prefreeze, it shouldn't peel off.

• **Freeze flat to save space.** Pour liquids such as stock or sauces into ziplock bags, then freeze flat. Store the frozen bags vertically (like a record collection) or horizontally (like stacked sweaters). A small plastic or metal bin can help line up all the bags.

• **Treat your freezer like an extension of your pantry.** A lot can go in there, but there's no need to stockpile. Pull from and add to the freezer as needed—daily, even!

• **Keep a list.** In restaurant kitchens, a *garde-manger* is the person who keeps tabs on everything in the giant fridges and freezers. You can be your own garde-manger by hanging an inventory of the freezer's contents on the fridge and updating it regularly.

• **Toss anything that's been in there for more than a year.** We try to use up frozen goods between 3 to 6 months postfreeze.

The Big Stock-Up: Our Tips for Shopping, Sourcing & Investing

Before buying bins, baskets, and sorters, consider this: Architects and landscape designers will wait to put formal pathways in a space until *informal* pathways have been created instinctually by its dwellers. Organizing your kitchen can benefit from the same line of thinking: *You* know best how you use it. What are your pathways? Let them guide you as you figure out what you really need. The tips that follow will help, too.

When You're Setting It Up

- **Figure out the pain points.** You need to define the issue before you can solve it, so start by thinking through the problems. For example: "My granola bars are all over the place." Or, "I'm losing things in the fridge." Or, "I can't find the tools I need."

- **You may already have what you need.** Slatted shelving on a kitchen cart is an easy way to line up pot lids. A crock or pitcher—or even a big jar—is ideal for a clutch of spoons by the stove. Need to wrangle your lemons and limes in the fridge? Nestle them in a pretty soup bowl.

- **Map it out before you buy.** Where in the kitchen will you keep your tools? Your pots? Your pot *lids*? Know what you need to buy before you buy it, and measure drawers and cabinets so you don't end up with crammed cupboards or containers that don't fit.

- **Get creative. And beware of anything that can't multitask.** A system that adapts to your needs (versus a collection of super-specific tools) is one you're unlikely to grow out of. A simple towel bar (yep, the kind you'd install in your bathroom) supplied with S-hooks makes a versatile, $20 catchall that looks good to boot.

- **You don't have to do it all at once.** You're creating a system and a routine—and those things naturally take some time to refine.

When It Comes Time to Buy

Seek out sturdy, utilitarian, frill-less bins, boxes, and baskets—ideally, they'll be easy to clean as well. Remember that you might already have the thing you need, so look around your home for tools first!

For more ideas, head to the Sourcebook on page 146.

- **Hardware stores or ULINE** for pegboards, S-hooks, cup hooks, and the like.

- **Home-goods stores (in-store or online)** for sleek wire baskets, heavy-duty plastic bins designed for the fridge and freezer, and specialized "organizers."

- **Office supply stores** for drawer dividers and organizers for small tools (that is, anything roughly pen size).

- **Thrift or antique stores** for vintage crocks, vases, baskets, and shelving.

- A few of our favorite sources for organized kitchens: **The Container Store** and **Bed, Bath & Beyond** for glass canisters, spice jars, wire baskets, and plain old inspiration; **Dymo** for label makers; **Muji** for simple plastic, bamboo, and metal baskets and dividers; and **IKEA** for lazy Susans, inexpensive kitchen carts and freestanding islands, handy crates, and rails, racks, and curtain wire (a nice alternative to a metal bar for hanging tools).

Where to Donate Everything You've Thoughtfully Cleared Out

There are heaps of organizations ready and eager to accept gently used kitchen tools, appliances, plates, and the like—and there are places to donate food you're not using, too.

- Take your cookbooks to your **local library.**

- Some **libraries** or **other community centers** lend out kitchen tools; call to see if your local places have this service. If not, consider offering to start one.

- **Senior centers, places of worship,** and **thrift stores** may accept lots of preloved items with life left in them—from linens and dishes to toasters and blenders. Call ahead to see what they can use.

- If you're renovating your kitchen, consider donating your appliances (as well as light fixtures, hardware, kitchen cabinets, and even flooring and building materials) to **Habitat for Humanity.** Many of their ReStore outlets offer free pickup for large items. (Likewise, consider shopping for your renovation at a ReStore.)

- Many branches of **Big Brothers Big Sisters** accept smaller household goods, like linens, dishes, and cookware (they'll even pick it up). Find a local chapter to see what they accept and schedule a pickup.

- To donate food, first make sure it hasn't expired and that any packaging is tightly sealed. Then:

  → Head to **FeedingAmerica.org** to find a food bank local to you.

  → Ask around at your **neighborhood places of worship, community centers,** and **shelters,** many of which also accept food donations.

  → Rally your friends (that is, convince them to clean out their own pantries) and have a mini food drive. Have a plan for where the food will go before collecting donations; it's worth calling ahead to make sure your chosen **food bank** or **community center** will accept them.

Our Cofounder
AMANDA HESSER'S
Tidy-as-Can-Be Kitchen

Amanda Hesser is known for her organized approach. Here, we got a glance at her airy, modern kitchen: Food52's very first test kitchen in the brand's early days. Amanda renovated her pantry in 2006, and the rest of the space in 2012—she's a fan of incremental renovations, design improvements in small doses—and created a home for everything. Dishware is stacked methodically in cabinets, cooking tasks get dedicated "stations," and tools live near where they'll be used. (We see you, stoveside utensil rack!)

→ **In my kitchen, the goal is to allow anyone to find what they need without digging around.** In the fridge, for example, I label everything and line up ingredients in a row (labels facing forward, open containers in the front). I also do a clean-out once a week, and bursts of maintenance in between.

→ **We have "stations" for our prep tasks**, like a spot near the fridge where we make toast and assemble drinks; a butcher-block counter across the kitchen with a pull-out garbage beneath, where our chopping is done; and a space beside the stove where prepped ingredients stay, next to a ceramic vessel with wooden spoons.

→ **My pantry is tall and has four levels of storage.** At the top: Canning jars, carafes, some wedding gifts (sorry, friends/family!), and larger serving pieces. Middle two: Canned and dry goods, spices, oils, vinegars, and heavier cookware that I use regularly. Bottom: Garbage bags, lightbulbs, candles, and vases.

→ There are a couple things in my kitchen that I'm still trying to figure out, like **how to organize my lids.** In my storage-container drawer, I line up lids inside a rectangular container. For pot lids, I have a rack inside of a deep pot-and-pan drawer. For my bowl lids—the circular kind that just flop around—I ordered an adjustable rack (kind of like a plate rack) that I'm hoping will solve all my problems.

I was raised by a master organizer: my mom. She vacuumed in straight lines, packed all of her clothes between layers of plastic, and ironed jeans. I do none of these things, but I definitely have her thirst for order and tidiness.

CHAPTER 4

Cooking

This is why we do all of the stocking, sorting, organizing, and cleaning—to spend time happily noodling around in the kitchen.

In this chapter, we talk A-to-Z skills, like how to safely use those knives you've picked up, or how to get a gorgeous, flavorful sear on tonight's steak. We've also got tips for building your confidence in the kitchen—and for making a cooking routine that's perfect for you. Stick with us and you'll have something good to eat every night of the week, plus delicious ways to use up your leftovers (no more sad desk lunches!).

30-Minute Cooking School: What You Need to Know to Cook Just About Anything

We really believe anyone—you! us! anyone!—can cook, and cook well. You don't need to go to culinary school or have an encyclopedic memory of recipes and techniques. You just need to have a few key tactics in your back pocket and use them regularly.

Here, we'll cover food safety, knife skills, and basic techniques for cooking on the stove or in the oven—plus, you'll find tips for efficiency, meal prepping, and recipe off-roading. Onward!

Food Safety: Clean & Clear

The most important part of cooking isn't meal planning or shopping or prepping—it's food safety. Food safety is the foundation of every meal you cook and eat, without which the most beautiful meal can quickly unravel. Luckily, most safety guidelines are either common sense or easy to remember. Here are the essentials.

- **Wash your hands**, every time you switch tasks, touch your face or hair, handle meat or fish, crack eggs. We really mean *all* the time, all over your hands, with soap and hot water, please.

- **Prevent cross-contamination.** Keep your cutting board and tools clean, too; wash with hot, soapy water between tasks and take special care after working with meat, seafood, or eggs. Wash and dry your produce thoroughly. And don't forget to clean your surfaces and sink regularly (learn how on page 136)!

- **Cool foods to room temp before storing.** Introducing still-warm food to the fridge or freezer can bring down the temperature of the entire environment, jeopardizing what's already in there.

- **Thaw foods quickly.** You can thaw your steaks or fillets of fish in the fridge in a day, but if you don't have that much time, try speed-thawing them on the counter: Place your frozen food in a freezer storage bag, squeeze out as much air as you can, and place the bag in a bowl of cold water. Change the water and turn the food every 30 minutes until thawed. Estimate 30 minutes per 1 pound of meat.

- **Cook meat thoroughly.** A handy-dandy instant-read kitchen thermometer is the best way to gauge doneness. You want 165°F for poultry, 160°F for ground meat, and 145°F for seafood, pork, and medium-rare beef and lamb. Without a thermometer, rely on your senses: Meat should be firm to the touch, like the pad of your thumb. Poultry should have no remaining pinkness, and fish should flake when prodded with a fork.

Knife Skills: The Sharpest Tools in the Drawer

Every cook needs both a sturdy, all-purpose chef's knife (more on that on page 4) and some know-how to really get chopping. Below is all the info you need to mince, slice, and dice your way to greatness.

Getting a Grip

The way you hold a knife matters. With a proper grip, you not only have better control of the blade but you also protect your fingers and your wrist.

Keep your workspace clear. As you work, move completed things off your cutting board—chopped onions to a prep bowl or a hot pan; peels into the compost—so you're never cramped.

Cut on a secure, even surface. Lay a damp paper or kitchen towel beneath your cutting board to keep it from moving. (For more on our cutting board faves, head to page 6.)

Keep your knife sharp. We've said it before and we'll say it again—a sharp knife is a safe knife. Pay regular visits to your local knife sharpener or hardware store, or learn to do it yourself. (There's no better teacher than YouTube for this!)

Your noncutting hand should be in a "claw" position, gripping the food you're cutting, with all the fingers (including the thumb) tucked toward your palm. As you cut, the knuckles of your noncutting "claw" should be flush with the knife's blade, creeping backward over the food as the knife chops; the food, meanwhile, should barely move.

Your "knife hand" (probably the one you write with) holds the handle while the thumb and forefinger grip the heel of the knife; you don't want to hold the handle with all five fingers. To get into position, think about how you'd go in for a handshake.

Chiffonade: Stack leaves of herbs or greens, roll them into a cigar shape lengthwise, and slice thinly across the cigar to create pretty ribbons. Roll your bundle of leaves as tightly as possible—it's best to do this in a few batches rather than all in one huge pile.

→ **Good for:** leafy herbs, like basil, or greens, like kale

Julienne/batonnet: Start by squaring off the thing you're cutting—slice four times around a carrot, for instance, to create four flat and even sides. Slice the squared-off item into thin planks, then stack a few planks at a time and slice them into long, skinny matchsticks.

→ **Good for:** firm, crisp foods, like cucumbers, carrots, jicama, peppers, and apples

Mince: Change your grip on the knife for this cut. Hold your noncutting hand on top of your knife and use it to help you ease the blade down in a quick rocking-chopping motion. You'll end up with teeny-tiny pieces, like a micro dice.

→ **Good for:** garlic, ginger, or woody herbs, like thyme or rosemary

Dice: Cut your ingredient in half to create a flat, even edge, especially if your ingredient is round. Next, place the food cut-side down, and cut long rectangles. Line the rectangles up side by side and cut across them to create cubes—small, medium, or large, per your recipe.

→ **Good for:** potatoes, carrots, celery, tomatoes, onions, or anything you want in small, even cubes

Slice: Let your noncutting hand creep backward as you slice into the ingredient. The cutting hand uses the full length of the blade. Slice *through* the object using a slight rocking motion on the front part of the knife, rather than separate cuts that go straight up and down at the blade's midsection.

→ **Good for:** radishes, scallions, onions, extra-thin pieces of anything

Roll cut: Hold the knife at a diagonal angle, slice your ingredient, and keep rolling it a quarter or a third after each slice. You get fun, unique shapes that are all roughly the same size.

→ **Good for:** long, thin cylindrical ingredients, like carrots, cucumbers, and zucchini

Stove Skills: The Frying Pan, the Fire & Beyond

The stove is where so much of what we think of as "cooking" happens—from flipping pancakes to simmering soup. To get in on the action, grab a pot or a pan and cozy up to your cooktop. These are the methods that will carry you through most recipes.

- **Sautéing** is our most frequently used method. It's a relatively gentle way to quickly cook food and build flavor. You use it, for example, to soften chopped onion or garlic before adding everything else to the pan.

  → Set a pan over medium or medium-high heat and then add a glug of cooking oil.

  → When the oil shimmers, add your ingredient and stir with tongs or a wooden spoon until softened.

  → To help an ingredient steam *while* being sautéed and accelerate the cooking, add a small splash of water to the pan.

- **Steaming** is an indirect and gentle way of cooking. We like it for quickly wilting softer greens, like spinach, or slowly cooking denser foods, like hardy winter squash.

  → Add a bit of water to a pot—more for bigger, longer-cooking items—and top off as needed to keep the pot from steaming itself dry.

  → Add your food to a steamer basket and set it over the water, making sure the water doesn't touch the food. Cover the pot.

  → Bring the water to a low simmer over medium or medium-low heat and steam until the food is tender.

- **Stir-frying** is extremely hot and fast. You use it to maximize browning on delicate and quick-cooking things, like green beans or shrimp.

  → Set a pan over high heat until it's very hot.

  → Add a glug of cooking oil that has a high smoke point, like peanut or safflower oil (olive oil will burn and taste bitter).

→ Toss in your ingredients and keep your face back to avoid getting spattered.

→ Stir with tongs or a wooden spoon almost constantly, pausing briefly to let the ingredients brown.

- **Braising** cooks food slowly and evenly in liquid, giving you falling-off-the-bone short ribs or melty, flavorful eggplant.

  → Set a heavy, ovenproof pot or pan with a lid until hot (Dutch ovens work great!) over medium-high heat.

  → Add your preferred oil. When it shimmers, brown your ingredients for a few minutes. Add enough liquid (like stock, crushed tomatoes, or wine) to submerge the food two-thirds of the way.

  → Bring to a boil; then cover and bake in a low oven (about 325°F) for between 20 minutes and a couple hours, until the ingredient is very tender.

- **Searing** is for aggressively browning food. You use it for steaks, big pieces of vegetables, and skin-on chicken thighs.

  → Set a heavy pan (we like cast iron) over high heat until very hot. While you wait, thoroughly pat your ingredients dry.

  → Add a glug of cooking oil that has a high smoke point, like peanut or safflower (no burnt, bitter, olive oil here!) and then add your ingredients with tongs.

  → Don't move or turn your items until they have a golden edge.

- **Poaching** cooks food gently in liquid, but for less time than a braise (and in a lot more liquid). You poach to get moist chicken breasts for chicken salad, tender and never-dry pieces of fish, or fragrant pears for dessert.

  → Put your poaching ingredient in a lidded pot, then add enough liquid—wine, water, olive oil, stock—to cover. You can add aromatics or whole spices, too.

  → Bring the liquid to a simmer over medium heat, turn the heat to very low, cover the pot, and cook until your ingredient is ultra-tender.

Oven Skills: Baking, Roasting & Knowing *Your* Oven Inside-Out

Every oven is a little different, and if you've been thwarted by a funny one—with a faulty door, haywire heating, or uneven footing that turns out lopsided cakes—you're in excellent company. The oven might *seem* to be a black box of mystery, but with some experimentation and know-how (an oven thermometer doesn't hurt, either), you'll be humming along in no time.

- **Know your oven.** Where is its heat element? Does it seem to run hot or cold? Most ovens are hottest at their bottom back corners. Keep this in mind as you aim for the best browning or most even baking.

- **The position of the racks matters.** If you want crisp chicken skin, place the pan on the top rack; it will receive heat reflected from the oven's roof. If you want cooked through, flaky piecrust, put the pie plate on the bottom rack, closest to the heat source.

- **Rotating your pans matters, too.** If you're baking, say, two trays of muffins simultaneously, plan to rotate them halfway through the baking time to ensure even cooking and browning. Switch the trays from top to bottom and rotate them from back to front.

- **To encourage browning**, increase the oven's temperature. Or preheat your sheet pan. Or make sure whatever you're cooking is totally dry, as moisture prevents browning.

- **To keep something from browning too quickly**, make a loose "tent" with aluminum foil and set it over the problem area.

- **What about broiling?** Your broiler lives on the roof of your oven or in a drawer beneath the oven. Use it when you want to brown or crisp something quickly without necessarily cooking it all the way through (say, a bubbly cheese crust on a baked lasagna). If the broiler is on the oven's roof, arrange the oven racks so that your pan will be 4 to 5 inches from the broiler. Broiling goes quickly, so watch closely!

- **When cooking without a recipe, remember these temps!** (And check out Your Kitchen Cheat Sheet on page 149 for any temperature conversions you may need.)

  → **200°F** keeps food warm and cozy without drying it out.

  → **325°F** cooks or braises a pot of beans or a fillet of fish loooow and sloooow.

  → **350°F** is your go-to for baking (Cakes! Cookies! Muffins!).

  → **425° to 450°F** is just right for roasting carrots or chicken legs with crisped edges and tender insides.

Myriad Tips & Tricks
for Savvy Cooking

We all have a friend whose table we love to eat at, whose kitchen we love to be in, and who seems like a cooking natural. A big part of that is confidence and practice. But your friend likely has their own set of tricks to make the job seamless. Here are some of ours, so you can start (or add to) your collection.

- **Revive wilty greens and slightly limp produce** by soaking them in an ice bath for 10 to 15 minutes.

- **Keep steamed or blanched vegetables crunchy and bright, bright green** by "shocking" them. Immediately after cooking, move them straight to an ice bath and let them sit until completely cool.

- **Prevent unwanted browning** on apples, pears, artichokes, and avocados by squeezing lemon juice onto any exposed cut surfaces. You can also soak the produce in a big bowl of lemon juice plus water for up to an hour at room temp, or a couple of hours in the fridge.

- **Easily peel . . .**
  - → **Garlic** by gently whacking a clove with the flat edge of your knife—the peel will come off.
  - → **Ginger** by scraping away the skin with the edge of a metal spoon.
  - → **Hard-boiled eggs** by gently cracking their shells after boiling and moving to an ice bath. The cool water sneaks under the shell, and helps the shell slip right off.

- **Keep your citrus zest together** by grating the fruit with the bottom side of your rasp facing up—this approach naturally collects all the zest up top.

- **Get a sticky, stuck-on lid off a jar** by wrapping a rubber band around the lid for a better grip. For even more grip, wrap a kitchen towel over around the rubber-banded lid and then twist.

- **Soften butter fast** by cutting it into thin pieces and letting it sit for 5 to 10 minutes. Or microwave the full stick in 10-second blasts, turning the butter onto each of its sides between zaps.

- **Hack a double-boiler** to melt chocolate (or make hollandaise, or cook other sauces gently) by setting a glass or metal heat-proof bowl over a saucepan filled with a few inches of water (when simmering, the water shouldn't reach the bottom of the bowl).

THE THING ABOUT ONIONS . . .

You thought we already taught you all there is to know about knife work! And we did (see page 96)—almost. See, dicing and mincing onions (and similar vegetables, like shallots) come with their own rules, thanks to all those layers. Halve an onion lengthwise, through its root end, leaving one end intact and slicing off the other end. Slip off the papery skin, and cut the onion into strips lengthwise, leaving that root end intact. Turn the onion so that the strips are perpendicular to your knife's blade, then slice across to dice. To mince, run your knife over the pieces of diced onion in a rock-chopping motion to get even smaller, finer pieces. Discard the root.

- **Halve lots of cherry tomatoes in one go** by positioning them between the lids of food-storage containers (like a sandwich!). Use your noncutting hand to gently but steadily keep the top lid in place while you slice between the lids and through the tomatoes with a serrated knife. Other small, round foods, like grapes or pitted olives, can get the same treatment.

- **Ensure evenly cooked meat** by bringing it to room temperature before cooking or grilling. The meat should feel just cool to the touch, but not cold, before it heads into the pan.

- **Boost your meat's flavor** and increase its tenderness by seasoning it with salt, pepper, and/or other spices, up to one day in advance. Keep anything with a skin you'd like to crisp up (like a whole chicken) uncovered during its overnight sit in the fridge; air circulating around the food will help dry it, and the drier it is, the crispier it will become.

- **Mimic a cup of buttermilk** for baked goods by using DIY soured milk instead—add a tablespoon of vinegar or lemon juice to a cup of cow's milk (or unsweetened nondairy milk) and let it sit for 10 minutes. The acid in this substitute will react with the baked good's leavener in the same way that buttermilk would.

- **To safely dispose of oil**, never pour it down the drain! Instead, let it cool slightly, then pour it into an empty wide-mouthed and lidded bottle, can, or jar. Keep the container in the freezer and pour excess oil into it whenever you need to. When the container is full, scoop out and discard the hardened fat and start over.

- **Retrieve a shard of eggshell** from your bowl of cracked eggs by wetting your fingers and then quickly and confidently grabbing it. The water keeps the whites from sticking to your hand.

PICKING THE RIGHT PAN

Now that you know your stove skills (see page 98), you should know that, yes, there are sometimes better pans for certain jobs. But how to know what to use for your dish? For extra-sticky or delicate tasks (like pan-frying tofu or scrambling eggs), go nonstick. For use over high heat (like deeply browning chicken thighs or charring stir-fried green beans), or when moving from stove to oven (as when braising or making a frittata), pick heavy cast-iron or enameled cast-iron vessels. For boiling water, sautéing, and the rest, stainless steel or aluminum will do you right.

Our Test Kitchen's Tips for Mastering the Art of Winging It

We love a recipe as much as the next cook—and we use them, get inspired by them, write them, and rewrite them. But there are times when we just want to set recipes aside and play. Winging it can make cooking exciting, and can reliably turn around a recipe that's gone off the rails a bit. Here, our test kitchen shows us how to veer from the course (and have fun!).

1. **Think about which flavors are already pals.** If you're searching for a missing flavor in your dinner, identify the flavors that are already present and then try to put your finger on a complementary one, based on where the dominant flavors are grown and used. Also consider any flavor combos you've encountered and loved in other recipes or at restaurants, and try mimicking those. For instance, you could pair garlic and butter, fish sauce and lime, star anise and scallions, tarragon and olive oil.

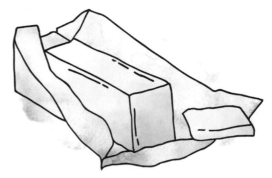

2. **Understand your ingredients.** If you know what kinds of ingredients fill certain roles in a dish—lemons and yogurt for acid, capers and soy sauce for salt, bread crumbs and sesame seeds for crunch, olive oil and avocado for richness, miso and mustard for savoriness, mayonnaise and butter for creaminess, honey and dried apricots for sweetness, and on and on—it's easy to freestyle or make swaps.

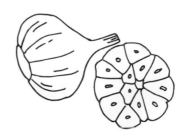

3. **Learn the big principles**, and you'll always know how to let loose. Experiment with different techniques using the same ingredient, or the same techniques using different ingredients. For example, if you pan-sear a fillet of fish skin-side down versus steaming it in a parchment-paper pouch in the oven, you get two completely different results. The same goes for roasting sweet potatoes versus string beans. But after you try a few things, you learn what techniques you like best for specific ingredients and can keep them in your arsenal for the future.

4. **Use a recipe as a launch pad.** Let it guide you for flavors, amounts, and timing, but tailor the rest—the ingredients, techniques, and the way the dish is served—to your own tastes.

5. **Trust your senses.** We rely on (and love!) our thermometers and buzzing timers, but our eyes, ears, nose, hands, and mouth are even more essential tools. This takes some practice, but with time, you'll be able to smell when garlic is browned, tap on the crust to gauge doneness for bread, or feel that a steak is medium-rare by just touching it.

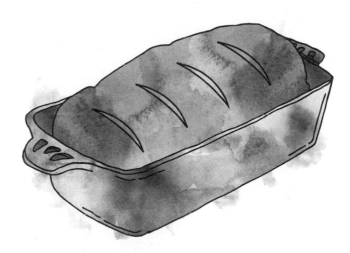

Mise en Place: What It Is, How to Do It & When You Should Throw It to the Wind

Fancy chefs like to throw these words around like confetti: *Meez, meez, meez*. But what does it actually mean? Adopted from French kitchens (which got many rituals and hierarchies from the French military—fun fact!), *mise en place* means "everything in its place." In the kitchen, here's what it looks like: Each ingredient in a recipe is fully cleaned, chopped, and portioned, usually into a brigade of small bowls, before the cooking happens. But although we love our mise, we actually don't use it *all* the time. Here's our advice.

When to Mise

- **For fast-paced recipes**, like anything being stir-fried, for example.

- **For new or especially challenging recipes**, so you can focus on the task at hand instead of readying the ingredients.

- **For recipes with lots of chopping**, so you can cook through the rest of the recipe without thinking about it.

- **For many baking recipes.** Whisk together the dry ingredients for muffins the night before—then add the wet ingredients, portion, and bake the next morning.

- **For cooking with kids.** Mise cuts down on messes and helps to keep the little ones' attention. Measure out or chop ingredients together in one session and cook in another.

- **For tonight's dinner!** Before you leave for work (or the night before), gather and prep your ingredients. Then all you have to do when you get home is assemble and cook.

When to Skip It

- **For recipes you know like the back of your hand**, you probably have all that prep handled.

- **For recipes with ample inactive cooking time.** Use the inactive time it takes to bake meat loaf, say, to chop greens for a side salad and make a dressing.

- **For recipes with a very short ingredient list or a simple technique.** Making a straightforward fried egg sandwich? No need to mise.

- **For those times when you're winging it.** It's your moment to shine.

WHAT ELSE TO MISE?

A group of *all* the stuff you need to make your dish, right next to your workstation—including the tools! Think of it as a kit: To stir together cookie dough, for example, prep your measured-out ingredients, lay parchment paper on your sheet pan, and keep a scooper at the ready. (Speaking of sheet pans, you can even use one to house your kit—it's easily movable for efficient transport to your workstation, and can collect dishes and scraps post-prep.)

3 Time-Saving Prep Tips, Straight from Our Test Kitchen

Our chef-in-residence Josh Cohen understands more than anyone the reasons behind meal prep: It reliably gives you a week's worth of lunches—or even just a head start on dinner. Here are Josh's three best tips for making the most out of prepping meals. With these, you can eat well (and fast!) all week and won't ever get bored.

1. **Rely on these four components.**

   → **Protein:** This can be just about anything—meat, beans, eggs. If meat, Josh recommends a fatty, sturdy cut (say, chicken thighs or braised pork shoulder).

   → **Vegetables:** Let whatever's in season determine what you roast that week. Josh cranks up the oven temperature to as high as 450°F so the vegetables get great char (read: great flavor) but stay crisp-tender inside. For bonus points: keep some fresh lettuce around to turn your mix-and-match items into salads or lettuce wraps.

   → **Starch:** Rice, quinoa, farro, barley, or potatoes are flexible and easygoing. After cooking, Josh spreads grains out on a sheet pan, so they cool quickly before being packed away.

   → **Sauce:** Even if it's as simple as oil, vinegar, and minced shallots shaken around in a jar, a zingy dressing makes anything better and unites a hodgepodge of ingredients.

2. **Season them simply.** This is the key to mixing and matching all week: Season with salt and maybe black pepper, and they'll pair easily with just about anything as the week goes on. A fridge full of shredded chicken, brown rice, flour tortillas, sautéed kale, roasted butternut squash, and yogurt can become (1) a rice bowl, (2) a chicken burrito, (3) killer fried rice, (4) a chopped salad, and (5) a hearty soup.

3. **Fear not the shortcut.** Pick and
    choose which components feel the
    most important for you to tackle,
    then let the supermarket take care
    of the rest. Grab a rotisserie chicken
    instead of roasting one yourself, use
    canned beans instead of dried, or
    cook up a pot of pasta instead of a
    more time-consuming grain.

If you prefer a here-and-there approach,
cook these "investments" when you're
feeling fresh, then portion and stash them
in the freezer. Think of them as your rainy-
day fund, which you can pull from as
needed and simply reheat—or transform!
Once thawed, plain cooked chickpeas, for
example, can be roasted till crunchy for
a snack, smashed into a tuna-like salad
for piling on sandwiches, puréed into
hummus, or stewed with tomatoes and
spices in a batch of chana masala.

- **Cooked beans** in their broth

- A hefty **pasta sauce** (say, marinara,
  Bolognese, or pork-shoulder ragu)

- **Puréed or mashed leftover roasted
  vegetables** (which'll turn into a creamy
  soup in no time)

- **Pizza dough** and/or **piecrust**

- **Large-format or labor-intensive
  meals** (enchiladas! dumplings! soups,
  stews, and chilis!)—enjoy half now and
  then freeze the rest for another time.

- A pot of **rice** or **another grain** (or
  uncooked riced cauliflower or broccoli).

How to Leave Cooking to Chance
(Do-It-Your-Way Menu Planning)

Need a zap of dinnertime inspiration? Just roll the dice to pass your cooking rut and collect $200—or, uh, pick an option or two from each category below, prep them at the start of the week, and jigsaw them together into delicious meals. Please play responsibly, and repeat as often as you'd like.

Protein
- roasted chicken
- seared steak
- cooked lentils
- roasted tofu
- simmered beans
- slow-roasted sturdy fish (like salmon or tuna)
- fried or boiled eggs

Veg
- sautéed hearty greens
- raw crunchy vegetables
- tender salad greens
- roasted veg
- steamed veg
- stir-fried veg

Starch
- crusty bread
- pasta
- potato wedges
- grains (like rice, quinoa, or farro)
- tortillas

Saucy Stuff
- olive oil and red wine vinegar
- a few shakes of hot sauce
- a dollop of Greek yogurt
- melted butter
- chopped fresh herbs
- a squeeze of lemon or lime
- green sauce or pesto

Snack
- roasted nuts
- cut-up fruit
- hummus and pita chips
- yogurt dip and crudités
- homemade trail mix
- dried fruit
- popcorn
- nut snack balls

Bonus!
- cookies
- muffins
- smoothie prep
- quick pickles
- granola
- homemade bread

A Meal-Prepping Mini Guide

A passion for meal prep has seized many a home cook (and us, too!). Not only does it streamline that last famished half hour between now and dinner, but it can also save money and slash food waste. It can even get you out of a cooking rut—maybe you bookmark a new recipe to try or turn your prepped components into a combo you've never had before. Commit to a couple of hours of menu planning, shopping, and cooking on any given Sunday, and you'll be ready to go for the week. Here's how to do it.

1. **Take stock of what's in your fridge and pantry.** What needs to be used up? Plan on working those things into the coming week's menu. (Also make a note of staples in short supply.)

2. **Assess your needs for the week ahead.** Maybe you want a few dinners to provide ample leftovers, plus an easy-to-grab breakfast, some lunch components, and a snack to ward off the 3 p.m. sleepies. Or maybe you just need some ready-to-go items to mix and match as the spirit moves you.

3. **Make a menu.** Plan the week down to every snack, or keep it loose by giving yourself a couple of anchors and add-ons to tide you over while you figure out the rest.

   → Your **anchors** are bigger, more substantial, and/or more time-consuming recipes that yield a generous amount of food and keep well—we're talking prime leftovers. *Think baked pasta, roast chicken, lentil soup, or that salmon recipe your friend sent you.*

   → Your **add-ons** are bits and pieces that round out your anchor to make a meal. They're usually quick to prepare and always versatile, so that they can be used in a variety of ways to bulk up or brighten a plate. *Think cooked grains; roasted, steamed, or raw chopped veg; vinaigrette; boiled eggs; or hummus.*

4. **Write your grocery list and head to the store.** Include the ingredients you need for the recipes you know you'll be making, plus your regular weekly staples. Leave yourself some space to be inspired by what you find at the store (like what's in season or on sale).

5. **Make a plan.** How much time can you devote to cooking today? Give yourself a timeline and write down what needs to get done. And don't forget that this is fun! Line up a couple of podcasts, put on a playlist to jam out to, or arrange a phone call with a pal.

6. **Cook away!** Start with the thing that needs the most amount of inactive time (perhaps one of your anchors) and use that downtime to do some nimble prep work. But unless your plan allows for it, there's no need to do it all in one day.

7. **Pack, pack, pack it up.** Grab those nice storage containers of yours (see page 25 for our faves) and put them to work. Label and date them with painter's tape and a permanent marker.

Food Stylist

SAMANTHA SENEVIRATNE'S

Ready-for-Anything Kitchen

It seems as if there's nothing Samantha Seneviratne can't do. She's written three books (*The New Sugar & Spice*, *Gluten-Free for Good*, and *The Joys of Baking*), brought her expert food styling to our photo studios, and contributed nostalgic recipes we can't stop making. Sam gave us a look into her lovely home kitchen, where she whips up weeknight meals and spends weekends baking her heart out. The galley-style setup features a roomy work area, generous counter and storage space for cooking tools (like her trusty stand mixer), and a window to let sunshine in.

→ **My favorite thing about my kitchen is the flooring.** The previous owner of my apartment put in these beautiful French tiles that make me feel happy every day. **I also love the amount of storage**—I have a lot of (too much!?) cooking equipment, and to have space for it all in New York City is exceptional. Last, **I love my wine fridge**, tucked under one of the counters. I don't usually keep enough wine to fill it, so I store nuts, coconut flakes, and different flours in there instead.

The best kitchen wisdom I've ever ever received? It's just food. I know that feeding people is a tough job—I feel totally deflated when my toddler refuses to eat. But if I take a deep breath and relax, I remember cooking's a pleasure. And he'll eat later. And so will I.

→ I make a handful of dishes regularly: beans and rice, veggies and eggs, breaded chicken, quickie paella, chickpea stew—but **I'm inspired by what's available at the Park Slope Food Co-op**, which I belong to. The produce selection there is wonderful and nudges me out of my routine.

→ I'm pretty into my **Instant Pot**. It cuts down on time significantly, plus, being able to put food on and leave the house is always a win.

→ **I love a cooking project that forces me to slow down and just be in the moment:** croissants, Danish pastries, sweet rolls (enriched doughs are my heaven). These recipes energize me and make me truly grateful to cook.

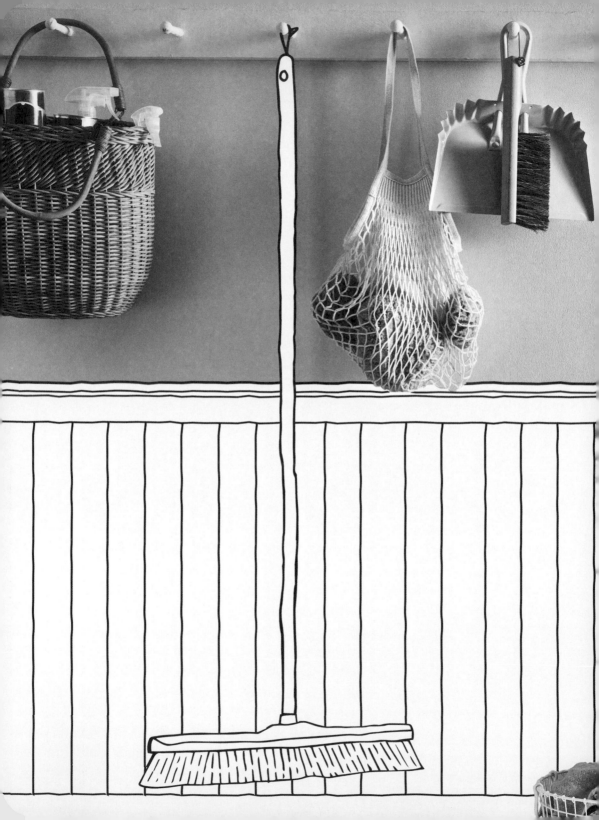

CHAPTER 5
Cleaning Up

A clean kitchen is a happy kitchen, there's no doubt about it. A tidy space looks and feels ready for anything—a rainy Saturday baking marathon, the frantic whirlwind of weekday breakfast-making, or the excitement before diving headfirst into whatever new recipe you're itching to try.

That's all well and good, but how to get the kitchen clean and keep it that way through the ins and outs of daily life? In this chapter, we cover the best cleaning supplies you can buy (and make!), and we give you the rundown on cleaning every shelf, surface, and cranny in your kitchen. We also throw in a handy guide for upkeep, plus easy ways to green your kitchen routine.

The Utility Closet:
Essential Tools & Supplies

The power of a few all-natural cleaners, rags, and scrubbers is truly amazing, and we turn to them to get super-fresh spaces. For our tools, we prefer gentle but sturdy nonplastic options, when available—they work better and last longer. For cleaners, we favor low-cost, all-natural, make-'em-in-5-minutes solutions, like the recipes on page 120. (It's true, you won't find bleach or almost any other commercial cleaner in this book.)

Tools for a Tip-Top Kitchen

- 5-gallon handled bucket
- Bags for trash, recycling, and composting
- Bottle brush
- Broom and/or hand broom
- Coir dish brush or scrubber
- Copper-wire scrubbers
- Dispensers and spray bottles for homemade cleaning supplies
- Dustpan
- Mini vacuum
- Mop with washable microfiber pads or disposable pads
- Nonabrasive sponges with a scrubby side
- Rags, retired kitchen towels, or cut-up out-of-commission T-shirts
- Rolls of recycled paper towels
- Stepstool
- Toothbrushes

Cleaning Supplies to Stock

- Baking soda
- Bar Keepers Friend and/or Bon Ami cleaning powders
- Citric acid
- Citrus peels (like lemon or orange)
- Distilled white vinegar
- Eco-friendly dish soap
- Eco-friendly dishwasher detergent
- Essential oils (citrus, lavender, tea tree)
- Kosher salt
- Lemons (whole)
- Liquid castile soap and/or Dr. Bronner's Sal Suds

Organizing Your Cleaning Crew

Storing your cleaning items in a thoughtful way is a must-do. You can't clean effectively if you can't see what you're working with! Luckily, we've got ideas for keeping everything in order.

Under the Sink

- **Dish risers** to finagle another level of storage.

- **Handled caddy or toolbox** for stashing essential solutions, brushes, and rags (and for toting them around).

- **Lazy Susan** for easy perusal of cleaning solutions.

- **Stackable lidded bins** for keeping extra dishwasher soap, compost bags, and sponges.

- **Wooden or wire crate** for corralling clean rags, scrubbers, and the like.

Elsewhere

- **Shaker-style peg rack:** Anything that can be hung (dustpans, baskets, buckets) or balanced (brooms, rolls of twine) will be happy here. It's an especially good solution for very small spaces, with little storage to speak of—just store your stuff all out in the open!

- **Storage closet:** If you have one—lucky!—your supplies have a natural home. Stackable containers (like wire or plastic bins) maximize storage of small things. Embrace vertical space as much as possible by using the closet's walls and door to hang tools, storage baskets, and bags.

- **Utility cart:** Think of it as a shelving unit on wheels. Pop baskets, bottles, and buckets up top and stash backup supplies below. S-hooks, hooked onto the cart's sides, can dangle for more hanging options. Roll the cart away to store in a closet or tuck it in a nook.

4 Essential DIY Potions to Make the Whole House Sparkle

They're cheap! They're better for the environment, with fewer freaky chemicals! You can funnel them into your own bottles and refill forever after! Best of all, they work all over the kitchen and home—and once they're made, they'll keep indefinitely. We'd pick these homemade solutions over the prefab stuff any day.

1 Best-Ever Dish Soap

For tough-on-grease, gentle-on-hands sudsing

2 parts room-temp water + 1 part Sal Suds or liquid castile soap + heaping spoonful of baking soda + big pinch of kosher salt

Stir well to combine in a glass measuring cup; pour into a dispenser bottle.

2 Sunshiney All-Purpose Spray

For glass surfaces and mirrors, stainless steel, ceramic tile, and more

1 part white vinegar + 1 part room-temp water + essential oils (citrus, eucalyptus, lavender, or tea tree) or citrus peels or eucalyptus leaves for antibacterial benefits

Shake well to combine in a spray bottle.

3 Gentle Giant Spray

For a cleaner that's gentle on surfaces that require special care

Room-temp water + drop or two of Sal Suds, liquid castile, or other liquid dish soap

Shake well to combine in a spray bottle.

4 Super-Scrubby Scouring Paste

For grungy sinks, grout, and cooked-on grease on pots, pans, or the stove top

2 parts baking soda + 1 part room-temp water

Stir well to combine in a bowl; then use or transfer to a jar.

The Big Stock-Up: Our Tips for Shopping, Sourcing & Investing

Cleaning supplies are truly about as utilitarian as it gets. But lots of supplies and tools (even brooms and spray bottles) can be beautiful. They're worth seeking out—especially if you'll be storing them in plain sight. When in doubt, opt for natural materials (wood, coir, metal, glass) over plastic. They look nicer and usually last longer, too. Here's where to shop for the cleaning stuff you'll need.

For more ideas about what to buy, head to the Sourcebook on page 146.

- The **Environmental Working Group** is an amazingly helpful online resource when deciding what cleaning products to buy. Their database of consumer guides details (and rates!) household products of all kinds, based on their ingredients and environmental impact.

- **Grocery stores or big-box, discount, or online retailers** for liquid castile soap, eco-friendly dish soap, sponges, recycled paper towels, kosher salt, lemons, citric acid (usually located near all the canning supplies), gallon-size jugs of white vinegar, and jumbo boxes of baking soda.

- **Hardware stores** for natural-fiber brooms and scrub brushes, Bar Keepers Friend, Bon Ami, buckets, and spray bottles and liquid dispensers.

- **IKEA** and **The Container Store** for genuinely nice-looking trash cans, utility carts, bins and crates, and straightforward large-scale storage racks.

- **Muji** for its simple, sleek cleaning system: a set of brushes, dusters, mop heads, and more that you can buy piecemeal, plus a handle that you screw the different heads onto, plus a storage case and a bucket. We're huge fans.

- **Restaurant supply stores** for spray bottles, liquid dispensers, and extra-absorbent terry cloth "bar mop" towels, which make perfect all-purpose rags.

HOW DO I KNOW MY KITCHEN PRODUCTS ARE ECO-FRIENDLY?

If the container lists the ingredients, that's a good sign. These terms on the packaging also point to greener options:

- **Phthalate-free**
- **Caustic-free**
- **Dye-free**
- **Phosphate-free**
- **Plant-based surfactants**
- **Biodegradable**

The Stove

If your kitchen is anything like ours, your stove gets worked *hard*—and is deserving of a little TLC. But just because it's well used doesn't mean it's hard to clean or requires heavy-duty cleaning products. Go forth to get out all the grit and grease.

Spot-clean

- **Wipe down the surface and range hood** with a hot, soapy sponge, or spray with Sunshiney All-Purpose Spray (see page 120) and wipe clean with a rag.
- **Wash the spoon rest** (if you have one).

Deep-clean a gas stove

- **Clean the grates and trays.** Make sure your stove is off and cooled down first. Remove burner grates and trays and pile them in the sink. Smear Super-Scrubby Scouring Paste (see page 120) onto the grates and trays, and let sit for 10 minutes. Wash with a hot, soapy sponge and dry thoroughly.
- **Clean the burner heads.** Wipe the burner with a damp rag, and then carefully use the point of a paper clip or safety pin to get into the narrow crevices and clogged ignition ports or burner holes (where the gas comes out). Wipe with a rag soaked in white vinegar to remove any bits and grease.

Deep-clean an electric stove

- **Clean the electric coils.** Give the coils a quick wipe with a damp rag. Then turn the burner to high for a few minutes to cook off any burnt-on food. Let cool completely, then disassemble the stove top by popping out the coils and the drip plates beneath them. Set them in the sink and use a dry toothbrush to get any residue off the coils—it should flake right off. Wipe clean.
- **Wash the drip plates.** Use a hot, soapy sponge to wash the plates thoroughly. To remove cooked-on food, generously apply Super-Scrubby Scouring Paste (see page 120) and let sit for 10 minutes before scrubbing it off with a sponge. Dry thoroughly. Ta-da!

For all other stoves, including glass-topped electric and induction stoves

- **Clean the stove top.** Use a hot, soapy sponge or Sunshiney All-Purpose Spray (see page 120) and a rag to clean the stove's surface (the space beneath the grates and trays, if your stove has them).
- **Tackle cooked-on food** by smearing it with Super-Scrubby Scouring Paste (see page 120) and leaving for 10 minutes before wiping clean. Dry well.

The Oven

Between spattering roast chickens, smoky broiler sessions, and crumbs that fall and turn to cinders, the oven cries out for a thorough scrub. From daily maintenance to the deepest of cleans, take it on with the following routine.

Spot-clean

- **Wipe down the handles, knobs, and front** with a hot, soapy sponge or with Sunshiney All-Purpose Spray (see page 120) and a rag.

Deep-clean

- **Incinerate.** If your oven has a self-cleaning cycle—which heats it to an extremely high temperature and burns off any stuck-on food—you can use that. All you have to do is sweep the remaining ash from the oven bottom at the end. But keep in mind that it will take several hours and the burning of the food often results in a strong smell.

- **Or . . . steam.** If the prospect of heating your oven to almost 1,000°F doesn't appeal, this may be more your speed. Simply place an oven-safe pan filled with water in the oven, set the temperature to 250° to 300°F, and leave it for up to an hour. You should then be able to wipe away much of the grime all over the oven—gently!

- **For really cooked-on stuff.** Sprinkle about a cup of baking soda along the bottom of the oven and spray with white vinegar to create a light foam; for the sides of the oven, smear on Super-Scrubby Scouring Paste (see page 120). Leave for 15 to 20 minutes and then use a damp sponge or rag to wipe it down. Rinse with hot water.

- **For crusty oven racks.** Line a work surface (or the floor!) with newspaper. Remove the racks from the oven, setting them on the newspaper, and use a toothbrush to get some of the cooked-on grime off. Liberally apply Super-Scrubby Scouring Paste to problem spots. Let sit for 15 to 20 minutes and then use a damp sponge or rag to wipe it off, scrubbing gently as needed. Rinse with hot water, dry, and replace the racks.

> **DANG IT—A SPILL!**
>
> If something spills over in the oven (it happens—*a lot*), cover the mess with kosher salt the moment you notice it. The salt will absorb the liquid, and you should be able to easily sweep the mess out once the oven is cool. If the spill is major (that is, more than a couple of drips and spatters), turn off the oven immediately to prevent a fire.

The Microwave

The spot where you heat bowls of Bolognese, mugs of coffee, *and* garlicky green beans is sure to get a little funky. Here's how to zap away the stickies, odors, and spatters.

Spot-clean

- **The outside.** Wipe down the handle and front with a hot, soapy sponge or Sunshiney All-Purpose Spray (see page 120) and a rag.

- **The inside.** The walls and turntable get a swipe with a hot, soapy sponge or Sunshiney All-Purpose Spray and a rag.

Deep-clean

- **Get steamy.** Fill a microwave-safe bowl (or a glass measuring cup!) halfway with water. Squeeze in the juice from a lemon and toss in the spent lemon halves, too. (The citric acid in the lemon is a natural degreaser.) Microwave on high until it comes to a boil, 90 seconds to 2 minutes. Let sit with the door closed for 3 minutes, then very carefully open.

- **Wipe away.** Remove (and reserve!) the bowl of lemon water and any glass turntable; you may need to use pot holders. Use a clean rag or a damp sponge to wipe the walls, ceiling, floor, and inside door, scrubbing gently if needed. Dip your sponge or rag in the hot lemon water if cooked-on spots need a little extra attention. Wash the turntable separately with hot, soapy water and dry thoroughly before replacing.

- **Final touches.** Use that hot lemony water and a rag to wipe down the microwave's handle and front.

The Fridge & Freezer

There's nothing quite like a tidy fridge and freezer, ready for action! Banish crumbs, spills, smells, and chaos like this.

Spot-clean the fridge

- **Wipe down handles and front** with a hot, soapy sponge or Sunshiney All-Purpose Spray (see page 120) and a rag.

- **Check the inside doors and shelves for spills**, then wipe down with a hot, soapy sponge or Sunshiney All-Purpose Spray and a rag.

- **Add a fresh, open box of baking soda** to the top shelf to absorb odors.

Deep-clean the fridge

- **The purge.** Remove everything and assess. Toss anything moldy or slimy and recycle any packaging you can. (Freeze or give away still-good but unused stuff.)

- **Wipe it down.** Remove drawers if you can and tap out any crumbs. Use a hot, soapy sponge or Sunshiney All-Purpose Spray (see page 120) and a rag to wipe them clean. Then tackle the shelves, starting at the top and working your way to the bottom. (Don't forget the fridge door and its rubber seals!) Thoroughly dry everything, then line the drawers with clean kitchen towels to help absorb excess moisture.

- **De-stick-ify.** Use a hot, soapy sponge to wipe down sticky or oily bottles and jars. Dry before replacing. If you use any fridge organizers or bins, give those the same treatment.

- **Reorganize everything.** Check out page 82 to learn what goes where.

- **Final touches.** Toss any old invitations, loved but dusty drawings, and the like from your fridge door. Use a hot, soapy sponge or Sunshiney All-Purpose Spray and a rag to wipe down the fridge's front and handle.

Spot-clean the freezer

- **Wipe down the handles and front** with a hot, soapy sponge or Sunshiney All-Purpose Spray (see page 120) and a rag.

- **Add a fresh box of baking soda** to the top shelf to suck up any freezer-burn smell.

Deep-clean the freezer

- **Pull it all out**, then decide what stays and what goes. Maybe turn some of the still-good stuff into tonight's dinner.

- **The big thaw.** If there's a major ice buildup, you'll want to unplug the fridge and defrost your freezer before wiping them down. If not, turn to your now-empty freezer with a warm, soapy rag in hand. Wipe away any ice buildup on the walls, shelves, and door. Run the rag under hot water any time it starts to seize up, but make sure it's just damp— not sopping wet!—to avoid creating ice buildup. Repeat with a warm, nonsoapy rag.

- **Sort and Return.** Keeping like with like is key (see page 85 for more tips).

- **Last but not least.** Use a hot, soapy sponge or a rag and Sunshiney All-Purpose Spray (see page 120) to wipe down the front and handle.

The Dishwasher

The thing that *does* the cleaning probably isn't at the top of your list of things to clean. But the dishwasher needs a periodic refreshing, just like any other tool—and the following steps will help it do its job better.

Spot-clean

- **The outside.** Wipe down the handle and front with a hot, soapy sponge or Sunshiney All-Purpose Spray (see page 120) and a rag.

- **The inside.** For a quick, hands-off refresh, run your (empty!) dishwasher's "sanitizing" or "high-temp wash" cycle.

Deep-clean

- **Remove the filter.** If you don't know where it is, consult your user manual (or Google your model) to learn how to disassemble it. Soak it in hot, soapy water, then scrub it with a dry toothbrush reserved for cleaning. Replace the filter.

- **Clean the cavity.** Spray the inside of the machine, including the racks and the inside part of the door, with Sunshiney All-Purpose Spray (see page 120) and let it sit for 10 minutes. Give everything a good scrub with a scrub brush.

- **Wash any removable parts**, like cutlery baskets, with hot, soapy water.

- **Rinse with vinegar.** To kill any lingering bacteria, place a dishwasher-safe container with a cup of white vinegar upright on the dishwasher's top rack, then run a hot cycle.

- **Finish with baking soda or citric acid.** To scrub out any odors or stains, generously sprinkle the bottom of the dishwasher's cavity with baking soda or citric acid, then run a hot cycle. Clean as a whistle!

Our Test Kitchen's Tips for Maximizing Your Dishwasher's Powers

If you're lucky enough to have a dishwasher, make it work as hard as it can. These prewash strategies all but guarantee dishware that comes out glinting cartoonishly. (And if your dishwasher happens to also be your dining partner, don't forget to give 'em a squeeze and say thanks.) Here are our test kitchen's tips—after all, we go through a *lot* of dishes.

- **Avoid loading up wood, cast-iron, aluminum, copper,** or other items that risk losing their finish. And no sharp knives, either—the dishwasher will dull their sharpness!

- **Scrape off food from dishes,** but no need to completely rinse. Your dishwasher soap needs something to cling to in order to be most effective.

- **Load from back to front.** It's not just efficient and space-saving, it also reduces the risk of accidental breakage. As for unloading, tackle it front to back, bottom rack to top rack.

- **Un-nestle silverware.** If your dishwasher has a silverware rack, group like with like to speed up unloading. If it has a caddy instead, shuffle your utensils to prevent spoons from, well, spooning. Dinner knives should point down, forks and spoons up for the most even cleaning.

- **Put bowls on the bottom rack,** facing the center, so water and soap can really get into them.

- **Add citric acid**—especially if your water is hard. "Hard" water (that is, water with high amounts of dissolved calcium and magnesium) can leave chalky or foggy white spots on your glassware. A tablespoon of citric acid added to your dishwasher's cavity solves the issue.

- **Wait to run the washer** until it's completely full to save energy and water.

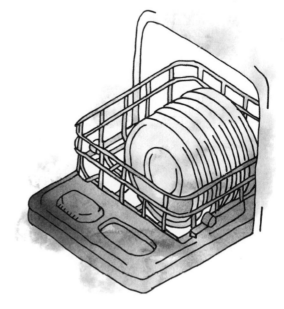

Pots & Pans

A cooked-on spot or a mysterious dark stripe isn't a death sentence for a favorite pot or pan. All it needs is a little attention. No matter what kind of pan you have and what kind of cleaning is in order, you can show it some love and restore the shine.

Stainless steel

SPOT-CLEAN

- **Wash your cookware with hot, soapy water and dry immediately** (this prevents water marks, too).

DEEP-CLEAN

- **To eliminate chalky white spots**, which are caused by calcium buildup in tap water, pour a 1:3 solution of white vinegar and water into the pan and bring to a boil over high heat. Let it cool and then wash and dry as normal.

- **For stuck-on food bits**, scrub the pot with a sponge to remove what you can; then fill the pot with enough soapy water to cover the food, bring to a boil, and scrape the bits away with a wooden spoon or copper scrubber. Let cool, then wash as usual with a hot, soapy sponge.

- **For discoloration from overheating** (this often looks rainbow-y), try washing your pan with white vinegar, or using the pot to cook a high-acid food, like tomato sauce (it'll be totally safe to eat!).

- **For burnt or burnished pans**, bring out the Bar Keepers Friend or Bon Ami. First rinse the pan under water, which will keep the Bar Keepers Friend in place. Then sprinkle on about a tablespoon of the cleaner and use the scrubby side of a damp sponge to work at the grime. Scrub vigorously, reminding yourself that this is your day's workout. Rinse and repeat if necessary.

Glass

SPOT-CLEAN

- **For a couple of pesky brown spots** that a sponge alone won't eliminate, make a batch of Super-Scrubby Scouring Paste (see page 120) and go to town. Rinse off the paste, wash the pan with soap and water, and dry thoroughly.

DEEP-CLEAN

- **For more stubborn stains**, bring out the Bar Keepers Friend or Bon Ami. Follow the same procedure as for burnt or burnished stainless-steel pans (at left).

Copper

SPOT-CLEAN

- **For a little blemish**, sprinkle on a bit of kosher salt and rub with the cut side of a lemon; for something larger, make a paste of baking soda and lemon juice and rub gently with a rag. Wash with soap and water and then dry thoroughly.

DEEP-CLEAN

- **For a truly *loved* copper pan**, coat the area with—bear with us—tomato paste or ketchup. (The acid is tough on tarnish!) Let sit for 5 minutes, rinse, wash with soap and water, and dry thoroughly.

Aluminum

SPOT-CLEAN

- **Wash with hot, soapy water** and dry immediately.

DEEP-CLEAN

- **Vigorously scrub** Super-Scrubby Scouring Paste (see page 120) all over, using the scrubby side of a sponge. Spray or wipe with white vinegar and let sit for a few minutes, then rinse and wash with hot, soapy water. Dry thoroughly.

Enamel or ceramic

SPOT-CLEAN

- **Wash with hot, soapy water.** Sponges and gentle scrub brushes are a-okay (but never any metal scrubbers!). Dry thoroughly.

DEEP-CLEAN

- **Cooked-on grime disappears in a snap** with a little elbow grease and your secret weapon: Bar Keepers Friend or Bon Ami. Follow the same procedures as for burnt or burnished stainless-steel pans (see opposite, left)—and don't forget the handles.

Cast iron

SPOT-CLEAN

- **Wipe out the pan with a hot (but not soapy!) sponge,** and give any problem spots a scrub with a coir or gentle copper scrubber, then rinse. *Never* soak the pan in water, or put it away damp. Instead, after rinsing, set it directly on the stove over medium heat and let it dry over the flame. If the pan seems parched—that is, not deep black and shiny—wipe it all over with a tiny bit of neutral oil and a clean rag.

DEEP-CLEAN

- **For a primer on refinishing and seasoning** a cast-iron pan, head to page 18.

The Head-Scratchers

If only our tools could talk and tell us what they need! We've gladly done some of the deciphering for you, to get the tricky ones sparkling again.

Wooden boards & tools

SPOT-CLEAN

- **To scrub out a stain,** add a bit of kosher salt to a small batch of Super-Scrubby Scouring Paste (see page 120). Dab it onto the stain, scrub in a circular motion using a rag or a brush, and rinse. Or try leaving the stained item in the sun for a few hours—it should help fade the stain.

- **To remove powerful odors** (lookin' at you, garlic), spray generously with white vinegar. (No spray bottle? Just dab the vinegar on with a kitchen towel.) Let sit 15 minutes and then wash thoroughly with hot soapy water. Let dry.

DEEP-CLEAN, OIL, AND/OR REFINISH

- **Start by sanding your cutting board or butcher block if it is truly dinged up.** We like a medium-grain paper (say, 320 grit). Sand along the wood's grain to freshen up the surface, but don't totally eliminate scratches—remember, it's supposed to look cut on! Brush off any dust.

- **Sprinkle kosher salt all over the board, and scrub** with the cut side of a lemon. (If you're cleaning a wooden spoon, make a paste of salt and lemon juice, then use a rag to rub it over the spoon.) Wipe off any excess salt with a rag.

- **Pour food-safe mineral oil all over the board** or spoon, then use a rag to massage it in, rubbing along the grain of the wood. Let the slicked-up wood sit for 10 minutes, then wipe away any excess oil. Ta-da!

Silicone baking mats & utensils

SPOT-CLEAN

- **After each use, wash thoroughly with a hot, soapy sponge,** then dry well, preferably out in the sun.

DEEP-CLEAN

- **When smelly or oily,** smear Super-Scrubby Scouring Paste (see page 120) all over it, then let sit for 10 minutes. Rinse clean; then dry. Alternatively, try giving it a soak in hot water dosed with a splash of white vinegar, then dry.

Stained linens

OIL-BASED STAINS

- **If the stain is from pesto or a curry**, say, wipe off as much of it as you can, then soak up the oil by patting on a bit of flour or cornstarch. Let it absorb, then dab (don't rub!) dish soap directly on to the flour. Toss the linen into the wash, using the warmest water you can for that particular fabric—or rinse it under a hot tap. If the stain remains after washing, repeat the process as needed, then dry.

OTHER PESKY STAINS

- **If the stain is from tomato sauce or red wine**, first flush the stain with boiling water, submerge it in a bowl of white vinegar for an hour, and wring out the fabric. If it persists, apply a nongel whitening toothpaste onto the area, then rub, rub, rub! (Because the toothpaste isn't in contact with the fabric for very long, it should only remove the stain, and not dye from the fabric. But if you're concerned, skip the toothpaste and try the Super-Scrubby Scouring Paste on page 120 instead.) Rinse and repeat as needed.

Silver, small & large

SMALL ITEMS

- **For cleaning a mess of utensils, small items, and servingware** (like your special-occasion silverware or estate-sale haul):
  - → Line a large casserole or baking dish with aluminum foil (or pick up a large disposable aluminum dish, like the kind you'd put in a steam tray).
  - → Sprinkle in a generous amount of baking soda.
  - → Add your items in a single layer, making sure each is touching the aluminum.
  - → Pour hot water over the silver, let it cool completely, then remove the silver and buff each piece dry with a soft rag. Magic! (Okay, science!)

LARGE ITEMS

- **For larger, awkwardly shaped, or single items** (like a pitcher): Smear on Super-Scrubby Scouring Paste (see page 120) with a rag; make sure you really massage it into the etchings and corners. Rinse clean under warm water, then buff dry with a soft rag.

Smelly dishes & food-storage containers

- **Soak plastic, glass, or glazed ceramics overnight** in a 2:1 solution of white vinegar and hot water. The next day, wash with soap and water, then dry.

Stand mixer

- **Remove and wash the attachments and bowl in hot, soapy water.** Dry thoroughly. Use a hot, soapy sponge or rag to wipe down the machine and (unplugged!) cord, then dry. Use a toothpick or pointy-ended skewer to excavate any trapped goop, dust, and residue. Be sure to remove the knob where you affix the mixer attachments, which hides a lot of gunk. Wipe clean with a damp rag.

Stained or smelly blender or food processor

- **Add a splash of white vinegar and a couple tablespoons of baking soda** to the bowl of your food processor or pitcher of your blender. Let the science experiment fizz and fizz.

- **Add about a cup of just-boiled water, then put on the lid,** leaving the feed tube or hole in the lid uncovered so that steam can escape. Blend for 30 seconds or so, pour out the solution and wash as usual with a hot, soapy sponge. Rinse thoroughly.

Spice or coffee grinder

- **Fill the bowl of the grinder with uncooked rice,** grind until the rice is powdery, and then empty the bowl and wipe clean with a damp rag. The rice will absorb the oil (and, hence, the odor!) from the coffee or spices.

> **BONUS: A TEST KITCHEN TRICK FOR DE-SMELLING A SMELLY KITCHEN**
>
> Simmer a small pot of equal parts white vinegar and water—plus a few strips of citrus peel, if you like—for half an hour. It should kill any leftover scents of frying oil, fish, or anything else you'd prefer your kitchen not smell like.

Pot & Pan Preventive Care: Our Test Kitchen's Tips for Avoiding Scrapes & Dings

Scratches are a drag for reasons beyond just aesthetics: They mess with your pan's patina, making it less nonstick (and possibly exposing you to harmful chemicals). The best way to avoid scratches is to know what causes them—and to steer clear. Take up our test kitchen's banner of preventive care.

For all pans

- Use gentle, nonabrasive cleaning materials and tools.
- If your pan has a grain (some metals, like stainless steel, have a grain just like wood), scrub *with it,* not against it.
- If you stack pans to store them, slip a clean rag or a paper towel in between.
- Dry thoroughly before putting away.
- Let the cookware cool completely before cleaning it—pouring cool water into a screaming-hot pan can damage the finish and even warp the shape.

For cast-iron pans

- Avoid using soap, which can strip that gorgeous seasoning you've worked so hard to build up!
- While you can use metal utensils and scrubbers on cast iron, use them gently to keep that seasoning where it is.

For enameled and nonstick cookware

- Never use metal tools or scrubbers on cookware! Seriously: no spatulas or tongs, no forks, no cutting in the pan. Pick wooden or silicone tools instead.

Counters (of All Sorts!)

Though we guide you through caring for all types of counters and backsplashes here, keep in mind that some materials—marble, granite, wood—require careful cleaning to avoid staining, scratching, or stripping of their sealant. Be sure to use a mild solution and skip abrasive cleaners, like baking soda or vinegar-based ones. Use only sponges, rags, or gentle scrub brushes. And seek out a professional's help to repair or maintain sealants.

Spot-clean

- **Wipe up crumbs** with a hot, soapy sponge or rag.

- **Put away unused tools** and appliances.

- **Clear accumulations** of papers, mail, and other "life things."

- As needed, **spray with Sunshiney All-Purpose Spray or Gentle Giant Spray** (see page 120), depending on what kind of counter you have, then wipe dry with a rag.

Deep-clean

- **Deeply de-crumb.** Remove everything—appliances, butcher blocks, trays, crocks, plants—from the counter. Wipe away crumbs, spray with Sunshiney All-Purpose Spray or Gentle Giant Spray (see page 120), depending on the counter material, and wipe dry.

- **Re-spiff a butcher block.** Head to page 130 for an in-depth guide to giving it some love.

- **Get good-as-new grout.** Make a batch of Super-Scrubby Scouring Paste (see page 120). Using a dry toothbrush reserved for cleaning or a dedicated sturdy scrub brush, vigorously scrub the grout with the paste. Then spritz on Sunshiney All-Purpose Spray or a 1:1 solution of white vinegar and water (it should foam a bunch) and let sit for 10 minutes. Scrub the grout again, then wipe clean and dry thoroughly.

- **Say good-bye to stains.** Does your counter have a "souvenir" from those juicy berries you ate yesterday? A batch of Super-Scrubby Scouring Paste does wonders on any kind of surface. Apply to the stain and let sit for 10 to 15 minutes, then gently wipe off—without scrubbing!—and rinse. You can also try using Bon Ami or Bar Keepers Friend. Sprinkle the powder onto a damp rag and then gently buff the stain.

The Sink

We turn our attention to the sink every day, right after we finish the dinner dishes. But it needs a regular scrub just like any other tool! It's also easy to add to your routine. Whether your kitchen sink is stainless steel, porcelain, ceramic, or otherwise, you might be surprised how *bright* a little elbow grease makes it.

Spot-clean

- **Clear the sink** and drying rack of dishes.

- **Run a hot, soapy sponge along the inside** of the sink. Use a scrub brush if necessary. Rinse with hot water.

- **Dry the faucet** and the countertop surrounding the sink with a clean rag or towel.

Deep-clean

- **Brighten porcelain or ceramic basins, or remove any stains from stainless steel.** Dry the sink. Spread a bit of Super-Scrubby Scouring Paste (see page 120) over the sink. Leave for 10 minutes, then scrub with a scrub brush or sponge. Rinse thoroughly.

- **Clean the faucet.** Spray with Sunshiney All-Purpose Spray (see page 120), then wipe dry with a rag. For hard-water stains, sprinkle with baking soda and scrub with a damp sponge or rag before wiping clean, rinsing, and drying.

- **Clear the drain.** Loosen up a clog by first pouring boiling water down the drain. Then, pack a full cup of baking soda into it, followed by a cup of white vinegar and a cup of water. After 15 minutes, pour boiling water down the drain to free the paste and—hopefully!—the clog. If not, time to call in a plumber.

- **Freshen the garbage disposal.** For a fresh-smelling, clog-free disposal, add a few big spoonfuls of baking soda and half a lemon to the disposal, then run hot water and turn your disposal on until the citrus has been broken up.

- **Clean the drying rack.** If the rack comes in multiple parts, separate them. Wash all of it with a hot, soapy sponge; soak anything smelly in a solution of water with a splash of white vinegar. Clean the countertop beneath the rack with Sunshiney All-Purpose Spray and a rag. Dry the parts of the rack and then reassemble.

The Floor

Your kitchen floor puts up with a lot—crumbs, spills, shoe scuffs, roving packs of dust bunnies. Treat it right! To do that, you need to know what your floor is made of and the sealants it's been treated with to avoid staining, scratching, or stripping them. Err on the side of extra-gentle cleaning solutions paired with the following tried-and-true techniques.

Spot-clean

- **Sweep high-traffic areas** and vacuum corners or crumby spots if needed.

Deep-clean

- **Sweep or vacuum the floor.** Remove any furniture or accessories (like rolling carts, stools, or floor mats), then sweep and/or vacuum thoroughly.

- **Mop the floor.** For this job, we prefer a washable microfiber mopping pad (see page 121). You'll also need a spray bottle filled with Sunshiney All-Purpose Spray or Gentle Giant Spray (see page 120), depending on what kind of floor you have. Spray and mop as you go in sections; when you're done, let air dry completely before returning the furniture. Rinse and wring out the microfiber pad and toss it in with your next load of laundry.

- **Tackle remaining sticky spots.** Spray or use a rag to saturate the gunk with Sunshiney All-Purpose Spray or Gentle Giant Spray, depending on what kind of floor you have. Use a scrub brush to work gently at the spot until it's gone, then let the area dry thoroughly.

The Pantry

It's one thing to have a tidy pantry; it's another to have a truly *clean* one. Why not have both? Find our detailed tips for organizing on page 76, and pair those with the steps below for a doubly spit-spot space.

Spot-clean

- **Return stray items** to their proper shelves.
- **Decant** any loose items.
- **Turn cans and jars so their labels face forward** for easy reading.

Deep-clean

- **Clear the decks.** Remove everything from the pantry. Wipe the shelves free of dust and crumbs with a rag, then spray with Sunshiney All-Purpose Spray (see page 120) and wipe dry.

- **Weed out your pantry items**, setting aside anything expired or forgotten to be tossed or donated (if unopened and before its expiration date).

- **Wipe right.** Use a hot, soapy sponge or rag to wipe clean any oily, sticky, or otherwise gunky bottles and jars.

- **Finishing touches.** Use Sunshiney All-Purpose Spray or Gentle Giant Spray (see page 120) and a clean rag to wipe down any cabinet fronts and handles.

Cabinets, Drawers & Shelves

Out of sight, out of mind; right? If only. Nooks, crannies, and other out-of-the-way areas—like your drawers, cabinets, and shelves—are happiest with regular upkeep. Whether spot-cleaning or really getting in there, here's how to get started.

Spot-clean

- **Give cabinet fronts and handles a once-over** with a hot, soapy sponge or the classic duo of Sunshiney All-Purpose Spray (see page 120) and a rag.

- **Tidy stacks and rows.** Reunite separate parts of things, like your stand mixer and its attachments.

Deep-clean

- **Cull and toss.** Remove everything from the cabinets, drawers, or shelves. Donate any unused or unloved items and toss broken ones (for how and how often we decide what tools go, see page 28).

- **Remove the drawers.** Tap out any dust or crumbs, then wipe out the inside with a rag and Sunshiney All-Purpose Spray (see page 120). Dry thoroughly.

- **Wipe away.** Dust the shelves with a rag, then spray with Sunshiney All-Purpose Spray and wipe dry with a clean rag. Use your Sunshiney All-Purpose Spray and rag to wipe clean cabinet fronts and handles.

- **Freshen up.** Wash or dust any dishware or tools that could use a refresh.

- **Good as new!** Replace your stuff, keeping frequently used items at eye-level or at the front and lesser-used items higher up and farther back.

Trash Talk

Everyone has it. Everyone *deals* with it. No one likes to talk about it. But trash is an important part of the kitchen ecosystem, and we want to make it easier to handle. To do this, we'd like to pose a challenge: Get a smaller trash bin than you think you need—say, 4 to 5 gallons—and redirect all your recyclables and compostables. Food scraps go in a 1-gallon compost bin, and recyclable paper, plastic, glass, and metals go in a 10-gallon recycling bin (or two, if paper's separate). We guarantee you'll take out the trash at least half as often, and it won't stink. Win, win!

That Smell Issue

A smaller trash can helps, and composting does, too. Beyond that, we've got some tips for minimizing the stink and giving your cans a good clean.

1. Start by taking out the trash!

2. If your can's in good shape, inside and out (not sticky, smelly, or dirty in any way), skip to step 7. But if it's not, follow steps 3 to 6 to deep-clean.

3. Squirt a bit of dish soap into the bottom of the bin, then add a few inches of hot water. Swirl vigorously, and let sit for 10 minutes. Swirl again, then dump.

4. If the inside is stained or grubby, use Sunshiney All-Purpose Spray (see page 120) and a rag or scrub brush to tend to the problem areas. Rinse again.

5. Wash the inside and outside of the lid with a hot, soapy sponge.

6. Dry all parts thoroughly, outside in the sun if possible.

7. Add a bit of baking soda to a plain mailing envelope, then seal it and toss the packet into the bottom of the bin. This will help absorb odors. (Really stinky things, like bones or seafood shells? Tuck them in the freezer until trash day.)

8. Fit with a new trash bag. You're done!

Recycle Like You Mean It

Seek out your state's or city's recycling guide so you know exactly what can be recycled. And remember: Most programs will only take items that are totally clean, so make sure you *really* wash out that peanut butter jar.

Start (& Keep!) Composting

If your city has a composting program, learn about what can be composted and where compost can be dropped off (like a farmers' market), or whether it can be picked up at your house. Keep your kitchen's compost bin within reach of your workstation, so you can add to it easily as you cook (store it in the freezer if you're worried about the smell). Of course, if you have a yard, you can compost yourself. Pick a spot to deposit your collection and add to it, turning the pile regularly. In a few months, you'll end up with happy soil to transfer to your garden beds.

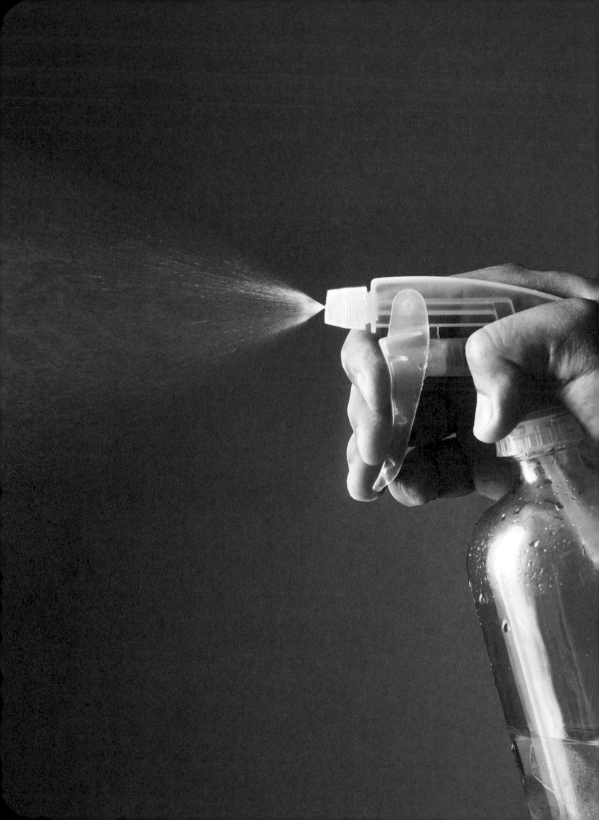

A Little-by-Little Schedule for a Squeaky-Clean Kitchen

We love the productive hum of chipping away at a checklist. Having a regular routine means we can all but go on autopilot. Here's how we keep the kitchen clean as a whistle—by day, week, and month. (Hint: Make a few copies to tape up on your fridge, so you can check things off as you go!)

EVERY DAY

☐ Wipe down counters.

☐ Wipe out the sink.

☐ Load and unload the dishwasher.

☐ Wipe down the stove top and range hood.

☐ Wash reusable water bottles.

EVERY WEEK

☐ Clean out the fridge.

☐ Take out the trash, compost, and recycling as needed.

☐ Sweep and/or vacuum the floor.

☐ Wipe down the fridge, freezer, dishwasher, microwave, and oven handles.

☐ Wipe down the sink faucet and handles and stove and oven knobs

☐ Wash kitchen towels, rags, and cloth napkins.

EVERY MONTH

☐ Mop the floor.

☐ Wipe down the cabinet fronts and handles.

☐ Oil wooden cutting boards and butcher blocks.

☐ Review and cull the contents of the freezer and pantry.

☐ Wipe down the inside of the microwave.

☐ Deep-clean the stove top.

☐ Empty the toaster of crumbs.

☐ Replace your sponges (biweekly).

☐ Sharpen your knives.

Restaurateur

JOANNE CHANG'S

Laid-Back Loft Kitchen

Joanne Chang has given us so much: The criminally tasty sticky buns at Flour, her bakeries, plus her illuminating cookbooks, *Baking with Less Sugar* and *Pastry Love*—to name a few. She also gave us a tour of the kitchen in her Boston loft. With limited counter space and storage, it makes the most of alternatives: A rolling cart, for instance, houses pots and pans, so closed cabinetry can corral smaller tools. Joanne manages to keep her kitchen uncluttered, thanks to a few restaurant-borrowed tips for a spruced-up space.

→ **We live in a loft, so the kitchen is part of the dining room, which is part of the living room.** I love how open it is. If I could, I'd add a hood—now, when I make a steak or stir-fry, the whole place gets smoky. I'd also love a bit more counter space. (Who wouldn't?)

→ **Cleaning as I go** is an important habit I picked up from working in restaurants. Between cooking tasks, I use a bench scraper to brush food scraps off the counter, so I can just sanitize at the end. (A towel alone gets really dirty, really fast.)

→ I love the meditative routine of **cleaning my 25-year-old KitchenAid stand mixer** with a toothpick. **Doing dishes** is the same; sometimes my husband, Christopher, and I will "fight" over who gets to do them (by hand!) because we both enjoy how calming it is.

→ When it's time to do a deep-clean, I begin by **pulling out every single plate and bowl and cup and can and jar.** Nothing is ever too grimy or dirty (since we clean as we go!) but things can get really messy, so I love to straighten everything out from time to time.

In the kitchen, I try not to rush. When I'm in a rush, I don't cook well, I don't enjoy it as much, the food doesn't shine—it's all wrong. The same goes for cleaning; I like to be deliberate.

Sourcebook: Our 52 Kitchen Favorites (In No Particular Order)

Only 52?! How could we choose? After much deliberation, here's our list of favorite tools, tableware, and other tidbits—the things we use and dearly love in our kitchens. These 52 items work hard, last long, and really look good doing it. We really think they're some of the best out there. (Hint: You can find many of them on Food52.com!)

Large Tools for Baking & Cooking

Cuisinart food processors

KitchenAid stand mixers and electric handheld mixers

Silpat nonstick baking mats

Staub enameled Dutch ovens and baking dishes

Smithey cast-iron skillets

GreenPan nonstick pans

Ballarini nonstick pans

Zojirushi rice cookers

Emile Henry ceramic baking dishes

Pyrex glass pie plates

Duralex 10-piece nested glass bowls

Nordic Ware aluminum sheet pans

Nordic Ware Bundt pans

John Boos butcher blocks

Demeyere stainless-steel pots and pans

Small Tools for Baking & Cooking

GIR silicone spatulas

OXO angled measuring cups

OXO cookie scoopers

OXO SteeL can openers

Microplane classic rasp zester-graters

Hawkins New York wooden spoons

Dot and Army flour-sack tea towels

Peugeot USelect pepper mills

Zwilling J. A. Henckels kitchen shears

Zwilling J. A. Henckels knives

Miyabi knives

Studiopatró linen aprons

Lamson metal fish spatula

Peg and Awl magnetic knife grabbers

Messermeister in-drawer knife blocks

Lovely Baking rolling pins

Baratza burr coffee grinders

Chemex pour-over coffee pots

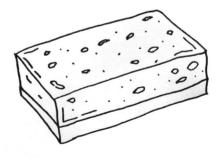

For Storage & Tidying

Black & Decker handheld vacuum

Bee's Wrap reusable food wraps

Specialty Bottle 4-ounce metal tins with window lids, for spices

Pyrex glass food-storage containers

Noaway countertop wood compost bins

Yamazaki Home wood-handled dish rack

Yamazaki Home wood-handled steel storage caddy

Dot and Army linen and cotton bowl-covers

Mepal microwavable nested storage bowls

Mepal airtight stackable storage containers

CapaBunga cheese vaults

For Serving

Hawkins New York linen napkins

Zojirushi thermal carafes

Soma glass water bottles

Mosser glass cake stands

Sawyer Ceramics French butter keeper

Bormioli Rocco stackable Bodega glasses

FisheyeCeramics gold-dipped pinch bowls

Dansk Kisco dinnerware

MADE BY US, MADE WITH YOU

Have you heard that Food52 has a line of products for the kitchen and home, designed by the very best cooks we know (that's you, our community!)? We do, and it's called Five Two. Together, we've made everything from cutting boards to cookware to the niftiest dish rack in town, and we're just getting started. Visit **Food52.com/ FiveTwo** to learn more about the line and snag a few gadgets for your own space.

Your Kitchen Cheat Sheet:
Handy Measurements & How-Tos

Halving or doubling a recipe? Making do with the tools and ingredients you've got? Getting ready to roast in an oven that measures degrees in Celsius? These charts are just what you need—and now you'll never, ever have to skip a recipe because you don't know the conversions.

They'll also help you if you're shopping for cookware measured in metrics—refer to them when you're stocking up.

Volume		
U.S.	**IMPERIAL**	**METRIC**
1 Tbsp (3 tsp)	½ fl oz	15 ml
2 Tbsp	1 fl oz	30 ml
¼ cup (4 Tbsp)	2 fl oz	60 ml
⅓ cup	2½ fl oz	80 ml
½ cup	4 fl oz	120 ml
⅔ cup	5 fl oz (¼ pint)	160 ml
¾ cup	6 fl oz	180 ml
1 cup	8 fl oz (½ pint)	240 ml
1¼ cups	10 fl oz	300 ml
2 cups	16 fl oz (1 pint)	480 ml
2½ cups	20 fl oz	600 ml
1 qt (4 cups)	32 fl oz (2 pints)	1 L
1½ qts (6 cups)	48 fl oz	1.4 L
4 qts	128 fl oz (1 gallon)	3.8 L
5 qts	176 fl oz	5.2 L
8 qts	256 fl oz (2 gallons)	7.6 L
10 qts	320 fl oz	9.5 L
12 qts	384 fl oz (3 gallons)	11.3 L

Baking Temperatures

FAHRENHEIT	CELSIUS/GAS MARK
250°F	120°C/gas mark ½
275°F	135°C/gas mark 1
300°F	150°C/gas mark 2
325°F	165°C/gas mark 3
350°F	175°C/gas mark 4
375°F	190°C/gas mark 5
400°F	200°C/gas mark 6
425°F	220°C/gas mark 7
450°F	230°C/gas mark 8
475°F	245°C/gas mark 9
500°F	260°C/gas mark 10

Length

INCH	METRIC
¼ inch	6 mm
½ inch	1.3 cm
¾ inch	2 cm
1 inch	2.5 cm
2 inches	5 cm
3 inches	7.5 cm
4 inches	10 cm
6 inches (½ foot)	15 cm
8 inches	20 cm
10 inches	25 cm
12 inches (1 foot)	30 cm
14 inches	36 cm

Water Temperature

	FAHRENHEIT	CELSIUS
Water freezes	32°F	0°C
Room temperature	68°F	20°C
Water boils	212°F	100°C

Weight

U.S./IMPERIAL	METRIC
½ oz	15 g
1 oz	30 g
2 oz	55 g
¼ lb	115 g
⅓ lb	150 g
½ lb	225 g
¾ lb	340 g
1 lb	450 g

Salt

Though we know we love salt, there are a whole lot of types—table salt, kosher salt, fancy flaky salt, to name a few—and it's not always clear when we should be using each type. Let's break it down. Here are the four most common types of salt, when to use them, and which are interchangeable.

TYPE OF SALT	WHEN TO USE IT	HOW TO SUBSTITUTE (1 TSP)
Table (with iodine)	Seasoning savory dishes, adding to baked goods	2 tsp Diamond Crystal brand kosher salt or 1 tsp Morton brand kosher salt
Kosher (Morton brand)	Seasoning savory dishes	1 tsp table salt or 2 tsp Diamond Crystal brand kosher salt
Kosher (Diamond Crystal brand)	Seasoning savory dishes	½ tsp table salt or ½ tsp Morton brand kosher salt
Sea (fine)	Seasoning savory dishes, adding to baked goods	2 tsp Diamond Crystal brand kosher salt or 1 tsp Morton brand kosher salt
Sea (flaked)	Sprinkling over dishes to finish	N/A

Conversion Formulas

TO CONVERT	MULTIPLY
Ounces to grams	Ounces by 28.35
Pounds to kilograms	Pounds by 0.454
Cups to liters	Cups by 0.236
Quarts to liters	Quarts by 0.946
Gallons to liters	Gallons by 3.785
Inches to centimeters	Inches by 2.54

Common Ingredients and Their Approximate Equivalents

1 cup all-purpose flour = 125 grams	1 cup whole-wheat flour = 113 grams
1 cup granulated sugar = 200 grams	1 cup brown sugar, firmly packed = 225 grams
1 stick butter = 4 oz = ½ cup = 8 tbsp = 113 grams	1 cup oil (vegetable, canola, or olive) = 200 grams (or 237 ml)

Converting Whole to Ground Spices

Have you ever thrown a bunch of whole spices into the spice grinder, hoping you get close to the amount you need, and then you're stuck with a ton of ground cardamom that you would rather not have sitting around? Let's not do that anymore—here's how to measure whole spices so you get just the right amount of the ground stuff.

SPICE TYPE	WHOLE SPICE EQUIVALENT	GROUND SPICE EQUIVALENT
Allspice	1 tsp allspice berries	1 tsp ground allspice
Black pepper	1 tsp peppercorns	1½ tsp ground black pepper
Cardamom	Approximately 12 pods, dehusked	1 tsp ground cardamom
Cinnamon	One 1½-inch stick	1 tsp ground cinnamon powder
Coriander	1 tsp coriander seeds	1¼ tsp ground coriander
Cumin	1 tsp cumin seeds	1¼ tsp ground cumin
Fennel	1 tsp fennel seeds	1¼ tsp ground fennel
Mustard seeds	1 tsp mustard seeds	1½ tsp ground mustard
Nutmeg	½ nutmeg	1 tsp ground nutmeg

Notes & Scribbles

Thank-Yous

This handy book is the product of ten years of Food52. That means a decade of thoughtful eating, joyful living, and gathering home and kitchen know-how alongside our test kitchen, brilliant team, and vibrant community of home cooks.

We couldn't have done it without any of those folks, but especially not Caroline Lange: For her quick wit and boundless creativity; for her super-friendly and imaginative writing; and for her savvy and charm when walking us through the kitchen. Caro, you make us want to—fearlessly!—drop everything and reorganize our pantry right away.

Many, many thanks to all the Food52ers whose wisdom is bottled up in these pages: Aja Aktay, Erin Alexander, Hana Asbrink, Posie Brien, Jaime Brockway, Marian Bull, The Canal House Cooks, Sarah Dickerman, Valerio Farris, Jojo Feld, Anna Francese Gass, Lindsay-Jean Hard, Sarah Jampel, Laura Kaesshaefer, Alex Kalita, Catherine Lamb, Derek Laughren, Karen Lo, Erin McDowell, Alice Medrich, Ella Quittner, Camryn Rabideau, Rémy Robert, Ashley Rodriguez, Bunny Schulman, Casey Simring, Amanda Sims, Ali Slagle, Leslie Stephens, Peter Themistocles, Louise de Verteuil, Brette Warshaw, Kristina Wasserman, Samantha Weiss-Hills, Sarah Whitman-Salkin, and Kenzi Wilbur.

Thank you to Food52's Team Books, who did so much to bring this project to life: Alexis Anthony, creative director and visionary, and Brinda Ayer, managing editor and chief word wrangler. Alexis, it's impressive enough that you sketched out this whole book in your head before we even knew all the words—down to every last pot lid and cup hook. But thank you, too, for sketching it out on paper (twice!), and for making it a reality so beautifully. Brinda, we can't thank you enough for your gentle but confident steering, and for your ability to simultaneously turn over every stone and see a many-armed project from above. This book is even better because of both of you.

Thanks also to Suzanne D'Amato, Joanna Sciarrino, and the Food52 editors. For your ideas and advice on just about everything—from putting together the puzzle pieces of each chapter to suggesting many funner ways to talk about scrubbing the stove.

Thanks to the creative team at Food52—Eddie Barrera, Anna Billingskog, Brooke Deonarine, and Amanda Widis—who worked their tails off to make these photos seem effortlessly beautiful. To Josh Cohen, Allison Bruns Buford, and the test kitchen team, thank you for answering all of our questions (there were many) and for making all the delicious food seen in here. A special shout-out goes to James Ransom and his assistant, Lara de la Torre, who figured out a way to magic a full kitchen in a tiny photo studio. And speaking of magic, thanks to our incredible illustrator, Nicole Belcher, whose drawings bring life and spark to just about every page.

Thousands of thanks to everyone who allowed us to pester them for interviews, who sent us photos and inventories of their fridges and pantries and pot racks and cleaning cupboards; our cofounders Merrill Stubbs and Amanda Hesser (whose own home kitchen was the original Food52 HQ); and the inimitable Allison Bruns Buford, Joanne Chang, Emily Connor, Eric Kim, Emma Laperruque, Kristen Miglore, Nik Sharma, and Samantha Seneviratne.

Endless, depthless gratitude to everyone who read this book's earliest bits and bobs and offered their thoughtful feedback: Adina Applebaum, Melissa Asselstine, Laura Booth, Shelby Brody, Gabrielle Davenport, Julia Dumaine, Isabella Giancarlo, Lauren Kolm, Nick Lange, Katy Lasell, Suze Myers, Mariana Robertson, and Alyson Yee. (And thanks again to Ali Slagle and Sarah Jampel for being among these early readers.)

We're very appreciative of Kari Stuart, agent extraordinaire, whose all-important guidance helped make this book happen. And to the incomparable team at Ten Speed Press: Thank you for sharing our love of order and organization, and for shepherding us as we collected our best lessons in this decidedly not-cookbook (that's, of course, all about cooking).

Most important, thank you once again to our community, for bringing us into your homes and giving us your tried-and-true tips, recipes, and stories over the years. You continually inspire us to make our kitchens the greatest they can be—even when there's flour all over the floor and we can't find our favorite wooden spoon.

Index

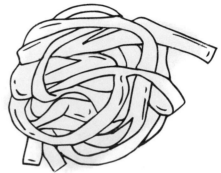

Published in the United States by Ten Speed Press, an imprint
of Random House, a division of Penguin Random House LLC, New York.
www.tenspeed.com

Ten Speed Press and the Ten Speed Press colophon are registered
trademarks of Penguin Random House LLC.

Library of Congress Cataloging-in-Publication Data
    Names: Ransom, James (Photographer), photographer.
    Title: Food52 your do-anything kitchen : the trusty guide to a
        smarter, tidier, happier space / editors of Food52 ; photography by
        James Ransom
    Description: Regular. | California : Ten Speed Press, 2020. | Includes
        bibliographical references and index.
    Identifiers: LCCN 2019039618| ISBN 9780399581564 (paperback) |
        ISBN 9780399581571 (epub)
    Subjects: LCSH: Cooking. | Home economics.
    Classification: LCC TX651 .F587 2020 | DDC 640—dc23 LC record
        available at https://lccn.loc.gov/2019039618

Trade Paperback ISBN: 978-0-399-58156-4
eBook ISBN: 978-0-399-58157-1

Printed in China

Writing and recipe development by Caroline Lange
Design by Lisa Schneller Bieser
Art direction by Alexis Anthony
Food styling by Anna Billingskog
Prop styling by Alexis Anthony, Brooke Deonarine, and Amanda Widis

10 9 8 7 6 5 4 3 2 1

First Edition